Perspectives on Suicide

Edited by James T. Clemons

Perspectives on Suicide

Sermons on Suicide

PERSPECTIVES ON SUICIDE

James T. Clemons
editor

Westminster/John Knox Press
Louisville, Kentucky

Book design by Gene Harris

First edition

Published by Westminster/John Knox Press
Louisville, Kentucky

PRINTED IN THE UNITED STATES OF AMERICA

9 8 7 6 5 4 3 2 1

Library of Congress Cataloging-in-Publication Data

Perspectives on suicide / James T. Clemons, editor. — 1st ed.
  p. cm.
 Includes bibliographical references.
 ISBN 0-664-25085-8

 1. Suicide. 2. Suicide—Religious aspects—Christianity.
3. Suicide—Moral and ethical aspects. 4. Suicide—Prevention.
I. Clemons, James T.
HV6545.P47 1990
362.2′8—dc20   89-16601
                    CIP

Contents

Preface

The idea for a book representing different perspectives on suicide came as I was preparing a workshop for the 1986 annual meeting of United Methodist Chaplains. Aware that this group included clergy serving in a variety of hospitals, homes, and penal institutions as well as all branches of the military, I decided they would benefit more from hearing the perspectives of three professionals in the fields of Bible, ethics, and pastoral care than they would from hearing the views of one person on all three topics.

While these plans were in progress, John Gibbs of the then John Knox Press called to ask if a recent *Christian Century* article I had written might be expanded into a book. My response was to suggest his consideration of the three perspectives to be presented to the chaplains' meeting later that spring. He encouraged me to submit the original papers and continued to offer invaluable encouragement and editorial direction in the intervening months. More recently, I have enjoyed and benefited from the editorial expertise of Harold Twiss of the Philadelphia office of Westminster/John Knox Press, who guided me through the final stages of the book's preparation.

To the three original papers have been added three others, somewhat revised, which were delivered to a "Working Conference on Suicide" held for a group of twenty-six United Methodist leaders in May 1987. The purpose of that three-day meeting was to draft a resolution on suicide to go to the 1988 General

Conference, the denomination's official policy-making body. The initial draft went through several revisions, each with further consultations by mail. Later, the proposal was endorsed unanimously by the denomination's Board of Church and Society. When approved for *The Book of Resolutions* by General Conference, it became the first official statement on suicide adopted by The United Methodist Church.

The last paper came at my request from Dr. Robert L. Kinast, following a luncheon discussion in my home with a process theologian and another process-oriented professor of pastoral care.

Editing this volume has given me many new insights into a most perplexing and urgent problem, as well as genuine personal pleasure. The result of all our efforts will, I trust, aid in the reduction of suicides, bring comfort and spiritual growth to those who have experienced that reality through the loss of family and friends, and move the church and other religious communities toward making a more informed faith response to this tragic crisis in our society.

J. T. C.

Perspectives on Suicide

Introduction

Few aspects of our society have gained attention over the past decade as dramatically as our attitudes and thoughts on suicide. Media coverage is almost unending, whether in reporting the sometimes bizarre cases of individual or group deaths, citing shocking statistics, featuring suicide on talk shows and panels, airing films and documentaries, or, occasionally, highlighting community efforts to prevent self-chosen deaths.

In addition to local groups, the Association of Lieutenant Governors has encouraged its members to work to prevent youth suicides in their states. Model programs include those begun under the former lieutenant governor of New York, Alfred B. DelBello, who later chaired the National Committee on Youth Suicide Prevention, and the present lieutenant governor of Arkansas, Winston Bryant.

At the federal level, former Secretary of Health and Human Services Margaret M. Heckler inaugurated a Task Force on Youth Suicide Prevention. This project, involving dozens of experts in various professions and including three national conferences, continued under Secretary Otis R. Bowen; the final report was published in August 1989. The report, in four volumes, is listed in the Bibliography. Two federal agencies charged with the ongoing responsibility of addressing the issue of suicide are the National Institute of Mental Health in Bethesda, Maryland, and the Centers for Disease Control in Atlanta.

One distressing fact has been the way this tragic event is occurring among segments of society where previously it was virtually unknown. While statistics are not as accurate as we would like them to be, often because of the persistent stigma attached to suicide, those figures we do have illustrate the extent of the current problem.

Some Shocking Statistics

While most media reports have focused on teenagers, in 1983 there were almost fifteen hundred more suicides in the 25-to-34 age range than among those 15 to 24. The death *rate* from suicide was also higher for the older age group, 16.3 vs. 12.4 per 100,000.

Although it was once thought that children should not be included in any study of suicide, presumably because they were considered immune from whatever causes suicide in young people and adults, recent studies have demonstrated that suicidal behavior in children is far from uncommon. Psychologists speak now of "early onset depression syndrome," which can lead to suicide attempts as early as age 3. Cases have been reported of children who by age 10 have made several attempts to end their lives. This raises the question of how many children's so-called accidental deaths, from falling, drowning, drugs, or running in front of cars, are in fact mislabeled. A particularly tragic dimension of adult suicide is the number of youngsters who are murdered by their parents before they themselves commit suicide.

Up to three and a half times more men commit suicide than do women, but about three times more women *attempt* suicide than do men. Among blacks, the ratio of men to women who commit suicide is even higher, underscoring the fact that the suicide rate among black males has been increasing sharply.

Native Americans have a high rate of suicide, given their relatively small numbers, although media attention has sometimes distorted the supposed increase.

In terms of professions, dentists and doctors have long ranked at the top among those who choose death, proving that wealth, education, and social standing are no guarantees against suicide. And within the past five years, the loss of many family farms has brought an increase in the number of suicides among farmers.

One television news program recently focused on suicides among police. Constant exposure to life-threatening situations, lack of public appreciation, low pay, long hours of boredom, frustration when those they arrest go free, and easy accessibility to destructive weapons were given as contributing factors.

Dick Ford, former Director of Jail Operations for the National Sheriffs' Association, has called the number of suicides in our jails and reformatories "a national disgrace." Faced with possible lawsuits for not providing adequate safety for their inmates, a few penal administrators have initiated training programs for their personnel in preventing and intervening in suicide attempts. Much more education along these lines is needed.

Also significant, though seldom mentioned in the news media, is the number of suicides among members of the military and their families. Studies and preventive measures have been initiated by military officers and implemented at times with the help of chaplains. One of the most detailed reports on military suicides was completed in 1987 under the direction of Charles McDowell and Audrey Wright. As their six-year analysis (1981 through 1986) of deaths by suicide among personnel of the U.S. Air Force stated, "Suicide continues to be a leading cause of mortality among active-duty USAF members, exceeded only by accidents and disease."[1] A Pentagon report cited in the *Washington Post* on January 21, 1989, said that while the number of deaths among military personnel who died between October 1, 1987, and September 30, 1988, was "the lowest annual total in more than a decade," the number of *suicides* in the same period rose to 257, ten more than the year before—the only category of deaths to show an increase during this time.

Veterans of the Vietnam conflict have been the subject of several studies on suicide, although questions have been raised about both the method of gathering the statistics and the interpretation of the results.

The highest rate of suicide for any group in the United States continues to be that of white males over the age of 65. In 1986 this rate was 24.1 per 100,000. Especially vulnerable are those who are in poor health and separated, divorced, or left as widowers. Loss of familiar surroundings often contributes to the depression that precedes many suicides.

When we think of these overwhelming figures, we must also keep in mind several other important factors: (1) the numbers of suicides at all age levels that go unreported; (2) the much larger number of persons who attempt suicide unsuccessfully (a ratio that runs at least as high as thirty to one among teenagers!); (3) the still larger number of people who exhibit suicidal behavior, even though they may never actually attempt it; (4) the incalculable number of "shaded" suicides, those people who choose death by refusing medicine or therapy, by overeating, or by indulging in other high-risk behavior without a sense of genuine gratification in doing so; (5) the large number of family and friends whose lives are affected, often by the stigma that society still puts on this form of death, by psychological problems of anger and guilt, and by legal and financial obligations; (6) the number of police, judicial, and health professionals involved, and (7) those members of society who, though relatively far removed from an actual suicide, are nevertheless affected legislatively and economically.

From this broad survey it becomes clear that suicide unquestionably touches a much larger portion of society than most of us would imagine. This in turn highlights the urgent need for a more focused and widespread response to the present crisis, particularly from religious communities, than we have seen so far.

The Personal Dimension

On a more personal level, suicide takes on a whole different range of meanings for those whose lives are affected when relatives and friends commit suicide or make the attempt. Professional caregivers, those who confront suicide in all its forms most frequently and directly, are themselves often affected by suicide even as they minister to others. Several ethical insights have come from nurses who encounter suicide victims and suicidal persons among their patients.

For most people, whatever their interest in the subject, suicide remains an enigma. Many questions—of physical, mental, and social causes, of religious belief, of history and social stigma, plus a myriad of ethical concerns—are woven around and through this single ever-present phenomenon. How do you define suicide? Is it a crime? A sin? Will my friend go to hell for taking her own life? What does the Bible really say? Is it a sign of mental illness? Is the tendency toward self-destructive behavior inherited? Why do people do it? Are all self-chosen deaths to be viewed the same way? Is there ever such a thing as a "good" suicide? How can it be prevented? How far should we impinge on another person's "right" to choose death? Must I intervene? What are the signs of suicidal behavior? What steps can be taken to prevent it? By me? By my religious community? Why is such a stigma put on survivors? How can I help children, spouses, and friends who survive?

Questions like these come quickly to mind whenever we confront the reality of suicide personally. One is struck immediately by the complexity of the problem. In spite of so much publicity, confusion still surrounds a reality that reaches into almost every segment of our society. Individuals and groups hardly know where to begin the enormous task of untangling fact from fiction, outworn creeds from critical reason, mature ethical responsibility from the fear of doing violence to the rights of others. This confusion exacts a terrible toll of pain, anguish, and frustration from millions of individuals. It likewise perpetuates archaic and unenforced laws in our states and widespread apathy in many religious communities.

Clarity on this immense and complex subject requires an overall view, best gained through a series of perspectives that will enable individuals and groups to see the central issues through the eyes of professionals in different fields. The term "perspectives" refers both to different points of view and to the ways they relate to one another. Each of the seven chapters here is written from a different angle by a person well-established in his or her own discipline. Together they provide an approach that is much needed but seldom found in the numerous works already published on suicide.

These chapters may best be appreciated by persons with a faith commitment, particularly a Christian one, but they should be helpful to others also. For example, regardless of the nature or degree of one's personal faith, medical and psychological facts about suicide, current statistics on its prevalence in society, ways of identifying suicidal behavior, and guidelines for making ethical decisions are pertinent to any serious consideration of the subject. All these topics, and other basic issues as well, are discussed here. Davidson and Shopshire speak of ethical matters. Wilbanks notes the importance of sociology and of pastoral care. Wogaman makes several references to biblical texts. Parker is aware of both ethical and sociological matters related to pastoral care, and Kinast comments on a philosophical worldview. Each of them, in one way or another, relies on the kinds of physiological, mental, and emotional data cited initially by Davidson.

While each chapter is directly related to the others, the order of their presentation has its own logic. First come examples of the best thoughts on current medical and psychological understandings, followed by the influence of sociology on contemporary approaches to understanding suicide. Over the past century, these two fields have provided more insight into suicide and more changes in attitude toward suicide than any others. One reason for different attitudes at the grass roots of church and society is the growing number of people who are no longer satisfied with the old notion that those who commit suicide are simply "out of their minds." True, this belief is still widely held, and the results of psychological studies are sometimes heatedly debated. Even so, some of our best hopes for reducing the number of suicides, providing care and comfort for those at risk, and effecting needed changes in society will come from the disciplines of medicine, psychology, and sociology.

Also instructive, even for those not actively involved in the Jewish or Christian faiths, is chapter 3 on the biblical evidence. A survey of what the Bible really says and does not say about suicide can be instructive in several ways. It would be hard to overestimate the role the church has played in shaping attitudes and thus in fostering legislation regarding suicide in most Western nations. It is those same deeply ingrained religious teachings that have created so much of the psychological guilt and social stigma that often result from self-chosen death. To gain insight into the biblical evidence is an important first step toward understanding the basis for many ethical principles of Western thought and many of the dynamics related to professional caregiving. Chapter 3 therefore describes each biblical account of suicide and attempted suicide. It also considers some of the many texts that have been used to justify or condemn the act by Jewish and Christian writers over the centuries.

There is one omission among the topics selected: a chapter on historical perspectives. The decision to forgo this important subject was based primarily on the fact that several good historical summaries are easily available. Among these, I recommend most highly the classic work by Henry Romilly Fedden, *Suicide: A Social and Historical Study.* Also quite helpful is the survey by Marilyn Harran in the *Encyclopedia of Religion.* My own contribution to this perspective has been presented as a history of the way biblical texts have been interpreted either to condemn or to condone suicide. This survey appears in my book *What Does the Bible Say About Suicide?* These and other works with useful historical summaries appear in an annotated list at the back of the book.

Anyone seriously interested in suicide very quickly confronts the question of ethics. Getting a handle on that subject—that is, seeing the problems for all concerned more clearly and identifying a framework and set of guidelines for addressing them—is the concern of chapters 4 and 5 on ethical perspectives. While the authors do not give a final yes or no to every moral question that might conceivably be asked about suicide, no one can hope to make an informed ethical decision on the subject without working through the kinds of serious considerations discussed in these two chapters.

Two widely publicized incidents point up how ethical problems confront us all as a nation. While many states have laws that make assisting another person to commit suicide a felony, both Gary Powers (the U2 pilot who was captured while on an overflight of the Soviet Union) and Oliver North (sentenced in the Iran-Contra affair) have stated publicly that they were offered lethal pills by officials of the federal government.

The last two chapters represent different perspectives on suicide in the area of pastoral care. Chapter 6—which includes a useful summary of the typical signs of suicidal behavior, as well as guidelines for how to respond in pastoral situations involving suicidal persons—is by a Protestant with much experience and training as a naval chaplain and local pastor. Chapter 7 is by a Roman Catholic professor oriented toward process theology.

Of all those who represent religious communities, professionals in the field of pastoral care have long provided the most significant ongoing care for suicidal persons and survivors. It is unfortunate that so often they are forced to work without benefit of a clear theological basis for their actions and without official statements of support from their respective denominations or governing bodies. The chapters by Parker and Kinast make a special contribution toward filling this void.

Suicide, in all its dimensions, continues to be a broad, intricate, and mysterious subject for human beings to contemplate. The problems cannot be solved by any one person, nor can they be fully discussed in a single volume. The present work is an approach for those wanting to see the subject more clearly, whether for personal enlightenment or for giving care and guidance to others. To these two groups, the book is dedicated.

NOTES

1. Charles P. McDowell and Audrey M. Wright, *Suicide Among Active-Duty USAF Members 1981–1986: A Six-Year Analysis* (Bolling Air Force Base, D.C.: HQ USAF Office of Special Investigations, August 1987).

1

Psychological Perspectives
Lucy Davidson

LUCY DAVIDSON practices psychiatry in Atlanta, where she is also clinical assistant professor of psychiatry at the Emory University School of Medicine. Her teaching experience ranges from work with second-graders to graduate students and psychiatry residents. She received her M.Ed. and Ed.S. degrees and developed language arts curriculum materials before returning to school for an M.D.

Davidson found medical school as an older student to be enormous fun—like getting to go to college again without having to be an adolescent. Her interest in suicide grew from work at the Centers for Disease Control as a psychiatric epidemiologist. There she focused on the problems of youth suicide and suicide clusters.

Davidson enjoys speaking to groups about suicide but says she sweats blood trying to write about it. She is presently a candidate in psychoanalytic training.

A suicide is a self-inflicted, intentional death. A suicide attempt is a nonlethal, self-inflicted act that has, as its intended outcome, death or the appearance of the willingness to die.

Suicide has become the eighth leading cause of death among Americans and the second leading cause among young people 15 to 24 years of age. While life-style changes and advances in health care have lessened the death toll from such traditional killers as cancer and heart disease, the proportion of lives lost through suicide has increased. Few people are untouched by suicide, either as caregivers to suicidal people, as surviving friends or family members of someone who has committed suicide, or as those who have personally struggled with suicidal feelings. The focus of this chapter is to present psychiatric and epidemiologic data on suicide to complement the theological perspective.

Identifying Suicidal Persons

Efforts to prevent suicide are based on our ability to identify persons at high risk for suicide and then to intervene effectively. Some characteristics of persons at increased risk for suicide are known from epidemiologic data—information derived from studies of large populations. For example, men are about three times as likely as women to attempt suicide. Whites have suicide rates nearly twice that of blacks. Thus, white males account for nearly 70 percent of all suicidal deaths in the United States. Rates for suicide among males peak in the young adult years and among the oldest age groups, while rates for females peak in midlife. Firearms are the most common method of suicide for both men and women. Self-poisoning (usually medication overdose) is the most common method of suicide attempt. Widowed or divorced persons are more likely to commit suicide than married or single persons. Suicide rates also vary geographically; they are higher in urban areas and in the western region of the United States. Suicides are most frequent in the spring, not during Christmas holidays as is widely assumed.[1] Persons who have previously attempted suicide are at increased risk for completing suicide.

Recently, suicides of young people have become a special focus of concern. Rates among those 15 to 24 years of age have nearly tripled in the past thirty-five years. Within this group the young adult (20 to 24) suicide rate is twice that of teenagers (15 to 19). Among young people, 89 percent of suicide victims are white males, and the ratio of male to female deaths is nearly 5 to 1. Young people also now use firearms as their most common method of suicide.[2]

Of course, one cannot discount the possibility of suicide in persons who do not fit the profile of those at high risk. A married thirty-year-old black woman who lives in the country and doesn't own a gun may still be ready to kill herself. The expression of intent to die supersedes any indicators of low risk. The wish to die may arise from situations of insufferable loss. Such losses may be tangible, as in a financial setback, or intangible, as in a loss of self-esteem. The loss may be actual, as in the death of a friend, or only potential, as in the feared dissolution of a marriage.

Highlighting demographic risk factors, however, can alert us to certain categories of people more likely to commit suicide. Other known risk factors include certain types of psychiatric illness—such as schizophrenia, depression and other mood disorders, alcoholism, and borderline personality disorder. Suicide generally occurs in the later stages of alcoholism, while it occurs earlier in the life course of depressive illnesses.[3] Clinical predictors associated with suicide among those with depressive illness include feelings of hopelessness, loss of pleasure and interest in usual activities, and the presence of psychotic delusions.[4] Alcoholics who commit suicide are likely to have made a recent serious suicide attempt, to have a history of several previous attempts, and to be in poor physical health.[5] The alcoholic suicide victim is likely to have recently disrupted a close interpersonal relationship.[6]

Certain periods during recovery from depressive illness or schizophrenic breaks are high-risk times for suicide. At the most severe stage of illness, the patient may be too apathetic and disorganized to carry out suicidal plans. Recovery, though, juxtaposes increasing energy and organizational capacity with the awareness of how painful and costly one's illness has been. Caregivers should not overlook the possibility of suicide at such times of apparent recovery and well-being.

Severe and chronic physical illnesses are also associated with suicide. Suicide rates are elevated among cancer patients and hemodialysis patients, as well as those with severe respiratory diseases.[7] However, one cannot assume that suicidal feelings are an inevitable part of even terminal illnesses. Dying cancer patients who were aware of their prognosis and had severe pain, disfigurement, or disability did not feel suicidal unless they also suffered from depression.[8] Feeling suicidal or wanting to die was associated with their clinical depression, not the physical illness itself. Overlooking treatable depressive illness among physically ill patients is a disservice, although unfortunately it is easy to do if one reasons, "Well, wouldn't you feel like throwing in the towel if you were that badly off?"

Pastoral counselors, clergy, and other church-related counselors may be sought out by persons with religious delusions. These delusions are fixed but false beliefs, not shared by peers of the same cultural and religious background. Because they represent impaired reality testing, the presence of religious delusions increases the risk of suicide. The particular content of the delusion may be even more ominous, as in delusions of unpardonable sin or psychotically magnified guilt, which may lead the client to injure himself or herself in an effort to atone. Religious delusions of being a specific holy figure, such as Mary, Jesus, or one of the saints, may culminate in suicide as the psychotic person kills himself or herself in an imagined act of martyrdom or vindication. The interviewer who is too timid to pursue questioning may miss these delusions or their import. Such questioning requires tactfulness and sensitivity or the client will perceive it as confrontation rather than clarification.

Prevalent myths about suicide make it harder for suicidal people to seek appropriate treatment. For instance, people fear that having suicidal thoughts is an indication that they are going crazy. Fear of losing one's mind can make a person withdraw even farther from potential caregivers and contributes to a sense of apathy and hopelessness that may be part of depressive illness. The suicidal person may fear being locked away, assuming that suicidal thoughts herald an inevitable decline to madness. Teenagers may be loath to bring up feelings that might stigmatize them or alienate them from their peers.

The potential caregiver may help keep the problem inaccessible in the mistaken belief that talking about suicide with a troubled person plants an idea, like a seed, that will grow until it overpowers the person's resistance. Such reluctance to broach the subject actually contributes to the suicidal person's fears that he or she is beyond help. Troubled people are usually relieved when a nonjudgmental caregiver inquires about their suicidal feelings. Even completed suicide is the fatal outcome of an ambivalent state. The suicidal person who comes to discuss these problems has enough desire to live to be at least indirectly seeking help to combat his or her suicidal impulses.

Asking questions about suicidal feelings first in general and then in more specific terms provides a broad range of data from which to assess potential lethality. Using a direct "Are you suicidal?" as an opener usually elicits a no. The person who feels hopeless, wishes to die, and believes that others would then be better off may answer no because he or she has no concrete suicide plan. The interviewer who begins empathically asking, "How bad do you feel?" and progresses to questions about hopelessness, not wanting to go on, wishing one were dead, wanting to die, wanting to kill oneself, and then inquires about possible suicidal plans and available means is much closer to understanding that person's potential for suicide.

Believing there are differences between people who are "talkers" and those who are "doers" establishes a false dichotomy that can have lethal consequences. People who make suicide threats or spontaneously discuss their suicidal feelings are not a population separate from those who go on to act on these self-destructive impulses. While most people who threaten suicide do not kill themselves, the threat itself indicates a high risk. The word "threat" implies manipulative, histrionic behavior. A suicide threat, though, may be a low-key, matter-of-fact statement, such as "I wish I were dead." Suicide threats are expressions both of a wish to die and of a wish to be prevented from killing oneself.

Misinformation about depression also hinders our efforts at suicide prevention. Too few people think of depression as a treatable illness. Friends, family, and the patient may all view depression as a character weakness. They see the depressed person as putting on an act or lacking willpower. Since depression is a common illness predisposing to suicide, its prompt treatment is a key factor in reducing the toll of self-inflicted deaths. Pharmacotherapy, especially antidepressant medication, in conjunction with psychotherapy is very effective in treating depressive illness.

Typical symptoms of depression include a persistently low

or sad mood. There may be brighter periods, but feeling sad, blue, or irritable predominates for at least two weeks. The depressed person may have crying spells. Typically, he or she loses interest and pleasure in usual activities and may withdraw socially. Concentration may be impaired, and the person may appear to be psychologically and physically slowed down. Some depressed people have physical changes, such as appetite or weight changes, poor sleep, or constipation. The person may brood or feel excessively guilty about some minor indiscretion. These symptoms may lead to feelings of worthlessness, hopelessness, and suicidality. Recognizing these symptoms as a pattern of depressive illness is an important step in getting help.

Behavioral indicators of impending suicide call for quick intervention. The suicidal person may be in touch with friends and family to say last good-byes. He or she may make atypical provisions for taking care of children or pets or give cherished possessions away. The person may make or revise a will, or suddenly make funeral and burial arrangements, and may procure the means of suicide, such as purchasing a gun or stockpiling medicines or even rehearsing the act. Special precautions may be taken to avoid discovery.

Suicidal people make an interviewer anxious and less observant of possible clues. Some of this anxiety stems from concerns about what to do if the person *is* actually suicidal. Do not leave the potentially suicidal person alone, even for a moment, until you are certain that he or she is not planning immediate action. Interview family members or friends to gain information the client may have edited or not perceived accurately. Assess the degree of social support available. Can family members transport the client to appointments, supervise medications, remove dangerous articles from the household, and by their involvement sustain the client through periods of hopelessness?

You may decide that the client can be treated outside of a hospital. Favorable indicators for this include the client's ability to establish rapport with the interviewer, a committed social support system, absence of psychosis or intoxication, and lack of a readily implemented suicide plan. Be sure that follow-up arrangements are definite; nonspecific referrals to a community mental health clinic or to lists of private-treatment providers are ineffective. Whenever possible, set the follow-up appointment before the client leaves the office. Telephoning the client to confirm arrangements increases the likelihood of compliance.

Preventing Suicide Clusters

Media attention has increased public awareness of suicide clusters: suicides grouped closely in time and space. Some element of contagion is believed to account for clustering, with one suicide in a "community"—such as a school system, a parish or congregation, a neighborhood, a Native American reservation, a military base, or a college campus—increasing the likelihood of subsequent deaths.[9]

People become exposed to these suicides either directly by knowing a victim or indirectly by word of mouth or through the media. This exposure is believed to contribute to suicide among vulnerable people through identification and modeling. Depression, psychosis, loss, poor self-esteem, and chronic feelings of emptiness are examples of psychological states contributing to such vulnerability.

Imitation alone cannot produce suicides. Factors contributing to imitative behavior include the attractiveness of the model, the ways that the potential victim may identify with similarities in his or her life situation, and the perceived rewards of the behavior.

Media coverage may dramatize aspects of the suicide that create pathos or make the decedent into a temporary celebrity. The actual amount of newspaper space accorded the death increases for younger victims and those who die violently.[10] After witnessing an elaborate funeral or school assembly, for example, young people may suspend their awareness that death is permanent and be swayed by fantasies of how others will miss them or be sorry for mistreating them.

The religious community has a central role in preventing the spread of suicide by this sort of contagion. The most effective means would be to prevent the first suicide. However, after a youthful suicide or suicide attempt has occurred, community preparedness means having a response planned. Ideally, this response represents the collaborative efforts of religious leaders, mental health professionals, community leaders, school system personnel, parents, and young people. Constructing the plan models the type of coordinated effort that is helpful after a suicide and establishes working relationships that are best forged before a crisis. When people know their assigned roles in the community's response, they are less anxious and thereby more capable of focusing their attention on the young people's needs.

Leaders should be aware of which types of person are likely to be at high risk for suicide in a cluster. These include both young people in the same social network as the decedent and those with previous suicidal behavior or poor baseline mental health. Those whose life histories or present circumstances parallel the victim's may identify more strongly with the decedent. Also at increased risk are young people with histories of impulsive or violent behavior. Simple and explicit ways to refer troubled youth for help during the crisis should be widely disseminated. The community plan should also provide opportunities for self-referral.

In planning the funeral with family members, clergy should strive to avoid intensifying the prestige that death may have accorded the young victim. Scheduling a funeral during school hours unfortunately suggests that suicide can stop the young people's world and make everyone take notice. Other youngsters can be helped to dis-identify with the decedent without abusing his or her character. Glorifying eulogies are a mistake. The person who committed suicide can be acknowledged as seriously disturbed and as someone who, unfortunately, had not yet found a way to work through his or her problems.

Small counseling groups can help young people understand that death is permanent and that the suicide victim will not gain satisfaction from any postmortem events. It is important to present suicide as a painfully permanent solution to temporary problems for which help is available. Young people should know that it is normal for such a death to lead many people to think about the issues of suicide; persistent and intrusive suicidal thoughts, however, are a signal that something important is troubling the young person, and he or she should seek help.

The religious community can be invaluable in addressing the needs of caregivers during the crisis. Those working to meet the needs of others after a suicide are under great pressure. Leaders, particularly religious leaders, may themselves feel isolated from peers as they care for others. They too need opportunities to ventilate feelings, exchange information, and seek reassurance and support. Provisions for increased contact with co-professionals during the crisis are also helpful.

Comforting Suicide Survivors

Suicide survivors are those intimates of the dead person who bear the anguish of his or her death. Misguided responses from the church community can intensify their pain. Many people who would otherwise be sensitive to the spiritual and practical needs of people in mourning withdraw from the family and friends of a suicide victim as if these people had some communicable disease. They may urge that survivors be replaced in positions of church leadership, especially if the survivor directed a youth group. In seeking reassurance that such a horrible thing cannot happen to someone they themselves love, otherwise nonjudgmental people can be quick to fault the survivors. "If you had done such-and-such, this might not have happened." Their own anxiety is assuaged at the cost of increasing the survivors' guilt. The suicide may be regarded as shameful, leaving survivors doubly bereft by losing the opportunity to talk over their grief with others. Pastoral attention to these psychological aspects of the church community's response can make a tremendous difference.

Summary

Educating ourselves about suicide enables us to increase our recognition of persons at high risk for suicide and to develop attitudes and approaches that increase the likelihood of helping potential victims. Higher-risk groups include male youths, women during midlife, and the elderly. Persons with substance-abuse problems, mood disorders, or other mental illnesses are more likely to commit suicide, as are those who threaten suicide or have made a previous suicide attempt. Potentially suicidal persons are more vulnerable during periods of loss, recovery from depression, and closeness in time to another suicide in the community.

Caregivers who recognize that feeling suicidal is a transient and treatable state can guide persons at risk toward available interventions. Awareness of depression as a treatable illness can prevent needless suffering. Knowing how and where to refer suicidal persons can decrease our anxiety in questioning troubled persons about their suicidal feelings and plans. Our acceptance of suicidal people as ill allows us to address the needs of survivors more empathically.

NOTES

1. Centers for Disease Control, *Suicide Surveillance, 1970–1980* (Washington, D.C.: U.S. Government Printing Office, 1985).

2. Centers for Disease Control, *Youth Suicide in the United States, 1970–1980* (Washington, D.C.: U.S. Government Printing Office, 1986).

3. R. M. A. Hirshfeld and L. Davidson, "Risk Factors for Suicide," in A. J. Frances and R. E. Hales, eds., *Review of Psychiatry, vol. 7* (Washington D.C.: American Psychiatric Press, 1988).

4. J. Fawcett et al., "Clinical Predictors of Suicide Patients with Major Affective Disorders: A Controlled Prospective Study," *American Journal of Psychiatry* 144:35–40 (1987); and A. T. Beck et al., "Hopelessness and Eventual Suicide: A 10-year Prospective Study of Patients Hospitalized with Suicidal Ideation," *American Journal of Psychiatry* 142:559–563 (1985).

5. J. A. Motto, "Suicide Risk Factors in Alcohol Abuse," *Suicide and Life-Threatening Behavior* 10:230–238 (1980); and M. Berglund, "Suicide in Alcoholism," *Archives of General Psychiatry* 41:888–889 (1954).

6. G. E. Murphy et al., "Suicide and Alcoholism: Interpersonal Loss Confirmed as a Predictor," *Archives of General Psychiatry* 36:65–69 (1979).

7. L. Davison, "Suicide and Violence in the Medical Setting," in Alan Stoudemire and Barry S. Fogel, eds., *Principles of Medical Psychiatry* (Orlando, Fla.: Grune & Stratton, 1987).

8. J. H. Brown et al., "Is It Normal for Terminally Ill Patients to Desire Death?" *American Journal of Psychiatry* 143:208–211 (1986).

9. L. Davidson and M. Gould, "Contagion as a Risk Factor for Youth Suicide," in U. S. Department of Health and Human Services, Report of the Secretary's Task Force on Youth Suicide, vol. 2, *Risk Factors for Youth Suicide* (Washington, D.C.: U.S. Government Printing Office, 1989).

10. D. Shepherd and B. M. Barraclaugh, "Suicide Reporting: Information or Entertainment?" *British Journal of Psychiatry* 132:283–287 (1978).

2

Sociological Perspectives
James M. Shopshire

JAMES M. SHOPSHIRE is a native of Atlanta, Georgia, where he received his undergraduate education at Clark College and his B.D. degree at Gammon Theological Seminary in the Inter-denominational Theological Center. Following five years of pastoral service in Des Moines, Iowa, he earned a Ph.D. at Northwestern University. He has served pastoral appointments in Atlanta, Georgia, and Chicago, Illinois, and worked in various capacities with a number of community, annual conference, and general church bodies. He is a clergy member of the Iowa Annual Conference of The United Methodist Church.

Shopshire served as a member and vice-chairperson for the 1985–88 General Commission for the study of Ministry of The United Methodist Church and continues as a member of that Commission in the 1989–92 quadrennium. Currently he is Professor of Sociology of Religion at Wesley Theological Seminary, director of the Wesley Institute of Urban Ministry, and academic coordinator of the Urban Ministries Track.

The startling social facts are a matter of record. Yet it is generally acknowledged that what is observed about suicide probably represents only the tip of the iceberg. Americans are committing suicide in record numbers. The reasons are many but elusive. Trends in recent years are toward increases among the young, slight decreases among the elderly, and increases among racial minorities, particularly young adult black males.

Given these trends, the news media regularly provide sensational reports on the occurrences of suicide. Seemingly related, or copy-cat, patterns and other shocking incidents are communicated in minute detail. In addition, television dramas and specials on suicide presented to the mass audience have provoked controversy as to whether media attention serves to prevent or encourage more suicides.

The intention here is, first, to inquire into the sociological implications of suicide by examining some of the pertinent concepts and theories in the disciplines of sociology and the sociology of religion and, second, to explore the possibilities for active responses through the resources of religious congregations. The classic formulations of Émile Durkheim are a good point of reference,[1] and a brief review of the researches of contemporary sociologists will provide important clarifications and correctives of Durkheim's pioneering work.

The interdisciplinary endeavors of the social sciences provide the backdrop for this discussion. Models of conflict theory and symbolic interaction theory are just two of many in the field of sociology that rely on interdisciplinary and holistic concepts and approaches to analysis. Included among these models should be an "experiential" approach to analysis, which draws on the historical and actual experiences of particular groups in society in order to understand and explain certain phenomena.[2] Such encompassing perspectives and approaches are basic to an adequate study of the phenomenon of suicide.

In the next pages, definitions, concepts, and theories of suicide come first, followed by a look at the demographics of suicide, as proposed by the question, "Who commits suicide and why?" The final section considers the socioreligious implications of the suicide rate and the suicide crisis in our society, focusing on the question, "What can the churches do and how?"

Definitions

The commonly understood definition of suicide is the taking of one's own life. More judgmentally, it is self-murder or self-homicide. It is the action of one whose intention is self-destruction. Suicide is comprised of "the special quality of being the deed of the victim . . . resulting from an act whose author is also the sufferer." It "is commonly conceived as a positive, violent action involving some muscular energy."[3]

In his early work on suicide, Durkheim pressed the case for a precise definition. In so doing he pointed out the limitations of commonly used nontechnical definitions. How are we to classify negative or passive actions that result in one's death? Is death resulting from the refusal to eat, for whatever reason, considered suicide? What of the iconoclast who commits high treason, known to be a capital crime calling for execution. Is that to be deemed a suicide? (Today we can add a number of other examples that strike closer to home, including the drug abuser, the smoker, and the regular consumer of saturated animal fats.) Durkheim, therefore, arrived at this definition: "The term suicide is applied to all cases of death resulting directly or indirectly from a positive or negative action of the victim."[4]

More recent studies of suicide acknowledge continuing problems both with definition and with statistical representations of suicides and the suicide rate. No one knows how many families and physicians seek to avoid the stigma that goes with a completed suicide by misrepresenting the truth. Coroners, for lack of evidence, sometimes refrain from recording a death as a suicide.[5] No one knows how many apparent accidents are in reality suicides. In the final analysis, no one really knows how many deaths result from passive, continuing long-term acts that are not counted as suicides. Indeed, the tip of the iceberg is all we can see.

Suicidologists, mental health professionals, and social workers who identify and care for suicidal persons have defined other terms: "completed suicide," "attempters" (who can be identified, to some degree, by certain characteristic or symptomatic behaviors), "survivors," "individuals at risk," and "families at risk."[6]

Approaches to the Study of Suicide

The theoretical foundations for the study of suicide as a sociological phenomenon were established by Durkheim in 1897. He viewed suicide as not just an individual phenomenon but a "collective phenomenon," which flows from the "collective consciousness" of the society. Individuals were not thought to become suicidal because of normal psychic or psychopathic states or because of "cosmic factors" or climatic conditions. The suicide rate was, for Durkheim, a phenomenon by itself and not just the sum of the individual acts of suicide in the group.[7]

Durkheim divided the causes of suicide into three types: "egoistic suicide," where the individual is inadequately integrated into the society; "altruistic suicide," in which the individual is overly integrated into the society; and "anomic suicide," where there is a breakdown or lack of regulation of the individual by the society. A fourth type, "fatalistic suicide"—the opposite of anomic suicide—was never fully developed. This type of suicide derives from what Durkheim called excessive regulation, "that of persons with futures pitilessly blocked and passions violently choked by oppressive discipline."[8]

Durkheim attempted to measure the quality of social integration present in societies or social groups and concluded that suicide varies inversely with the degree of integration.[9] Strongly integrated groups "demonstrated" a low suicide rate as compared with groups seen as less well integrated or in the process of disintegration. Religion reduced suicide by its collective function of fostering intensified relationships, strong social bonding, and shared values. This effect was not dependent on the culture of the group or its internal sentiments, such as the theological orientation of a religious group, Durkheim said; rather, it was solely a result of the degree of social integration. Durkheim's famous theory that Catholic countries in Europe had lower suicide rates than Protestant countries was based on his conclusion that the Catholic church and Catholic areas had stronger social bonds than Protestant churches and predominantly Protestant areas.

Some of Durkheim's data and conclusions were called into question as early as 1954, and recent sociological studies have also sought to correct his work. Looking at data on church membership, suicide, and homicide in larger American cities for the early years of the twentieth century, Bainbridge and Stark did not find Protestant-Catholic differences. As a result they discount Durkheim's finding—"There never was a real

Catholic-Protestant effect"[10]—and present data and specific findings to this effect:

1. Social integration does prevent suicide, as Durkheim said it did.
2. Church membership does prevent suicide, as Durkheim's theory seems to imply, even if he dismissed religious effects per se.
3. The effect of religion is probably more than merely its ability to provide social integration, contrary to Durkheim's view that religion is nothing but community.
4. Social integration and religion are not related to homicide in our data, contrary to Durkheim's prediction.
5. Catholicism does not prevent suicide any more successfully than does Protestantism, contrary to one of Durkheim's most influential hypotheses.
6. Protestantism does not prevent homicide any more successfully than does Catholicism.

This completes a very serious case against Durkheim's entire understanding of Christian religion.[11]

Another paper, by Stark, Doyle, and Rushing, reports significant observations based on an empirical test of Durkheim's major assertions using contemporary data from American Standard Metropolitan Statistical Areas (SMSA's, now called MSA's). While acknowledging his contribution to the discipline of sociology, the writers found Durkheim to be "amazingly uninformed and misleading about elementary features of religion in 19th-century Europe."[12] Although he maintained there were no differences between Protestants and Catholics on the theological understanding of suicide—that "they both prohibit suicide with equal emphasis"—Durkheim failed to observe that the "Roman Catholic Church imposed vastly heavier theological and social sanctions against suicide than did most Protestant groups."[13]

Durkheim developed serious contradictions concerning religion and its integrative social function. Like Marx, he saw religion as epiphenomenon, as superstructure, a reification or symbolization of society itself, a representation of real or objective social arrangements. In another publication he maintained that religion has the power to unite its adherents "into one single moral community called a Church."[14] In *Suicide* he denies that religion as religion can have any power to affect the rate of suicide, except as a strong social integrator. He attempts to have it both ways, and therein lies a problem.

In another instance, Durkheim apparently glossed over the case of Great Britain, a predominantly Protestant nation, pluralistic and therefore (by his definition) having a weaker degree of social integration. Yet it had a lower suicide rate than that reported for most of the Catholic nations and regions on which Durkheim presented data. Stark, Doyle, and Rushing make the point:

> If pluralism must result in a low degree of social integration, as Durkheim claimed, then the British case is even more devastating than he knew (or acknowledged). For at the time Durkheim wrote, only a minority (30%) of British church members were Anglicans (Currie et al., 1977). Surely the presence of a multitude of non-conforming Protestant bodies in Britain and the many conflicts (including civil war) over religious pluralism were not state secrets unknown on the continent. But Durkheim seemed innocent of the rapid and amazing growth of Methodism, of the existence of Scottish Presbyterianism, to say nothing of the many other groups such as Baptists and Quakers.[15]

The researchers came to this conclusion:

> The data suggest Durkheim was quite right to stress the importance of social integration in explaining suicide. Using population turnover as an inferential measure of the density and intensity of interpersonal relations in metropolitan areas, we found very substantial effects on suicide—effects in accord with the basic arguments developed in *Suicide*. . . . But Durkheim was quite wrong to claim that religious effects on suicide are no more than a reflection of social integration. We have seen that his arguments against religious effects per se were faulty and his factual claims about religion in late 19th-century Europe were often dead wrong. Moreover, our data reveal a strong religious effect on suicide independent of social integration.[16]

The conclusions of several other researchers are essentially the same. Durkheim was an important pioneer in the field of sociology, but he made errors that invalidate some of his conclusions. In a seminal paper on suicide in America, K. D. Breault reviews the significant current social scientific literature on suicide. One of the important functions of Breault's paper is to place in proper perspective both the solid contributions and the flaws in the continuing research. This author "critiques the critiques" on religious integration and suicide in a balanced and informative manner, simply noting that

> a number of researchers have moved away from Durkheim's denominational operationalization of this theory of religious integration and have begun to test the basic theory itself, that religion in general provides protection from suicide. Many of these tests are flawed, however, for a variety of theoretical and methodological reasons.[17]

The above notwithstanding, the conclusions of Bainbridge and Stark are informative for the purposes of this discussion:

> Durkheim's underlying theory that loss of social bonds leads to various kinds of deviance including suicide is confirmed, however. Religion, whether Protestant or Catholic, has great power to prevent suicide, partly because it represents community and the sustaining power of human relationships. But religion appears to have an extra ability to prevent suicide, quite apart from the social integration it provides, a truly *religious factor.*
>
> We propose that religion has the *power to comfort* people who otherwise would be plunged into the depths of despair, a power relevant for suicide but not for homicide. Religion provides a measure of hope and the feeling that one's present sufferings are meaningful, compensating to some extent for deprivations and difficulties experienced in the mundane world (Stark and Bainbridge, 1979, 1980). Sustained by religious faith, some potential suicides, whether Protestant or Catholic, will endure their suffering and live until better days.[18]

Other sources of intensive study of the suicide phenomenon include psychological and psychiatric caregivers and related associations, educational and school-related associations, government and other secular agencies, and, to some extent, the general agencies of churches and religious organizations. As James Clemons has pointedly asserted, "the church experiences a theological lag in the matter of suicide." He continues:

"It is time for the whole church—laity, sociologists, psychologists, as well as theologians, church historians, biblical scholars, chaplains, and preachers—to address the matter in terms that speak to today's changing situations, statistics, and attitudes."[19]

Thus the emerging sociological perspectives that command our attention are not the products of any narrow disciplinary exercise. The most helpful perspectives point to the interaction of individual, social structural, and cultural factors. They are fluid, open, and interdisciplinary views that recognize the interaction of the discipline of sociology with other approaches in dealing with the issue of suicide. The emphasis is on social science, which seeks to raise the appropriate questions and provide insights, understandings, and explanations that inform and shape the response of the churches to the suicide crisis.

The Demographics: Who Commits Suicide and Why?

Suicide cuts across all age, sex, occupational, religious, racial, and other groups. Yet, age, sex, and race figures provide the most revealing patterns and trends with reference to the United States.

Age

The elderly. People over 60 years of age accounted for 23 percent of all suicides in 1980, although they were only 16 percent of the population. Older adults are at highest risk for death by suicide, although the suicide rate per 100,000 population for the elderly shows a slight decrease in recent years. In 1983, persons over 65 years of age comprised 11.7 percent of the population and 18.7 percent of the suicides.[20] In 1986, persons 65 years of age and older represented 12.1 percent of the population with a 24.1 suicide rate per 100,000 population.[21] The provisional census data for 1987 indicate that the percentage of persons over 65 years of age continued to increase to 12.2 percent of the total U.S. population, but there was a slight decline in the rate of suicides per 100,000 of this group to 23.7 for the year.[22]

Elderly white males are most likely to commit suicide. Suicide among the elderly is usually not impulsive. Among the more obvious contributing factors are physical decline, loss of close kin and loved ones through death or abandonment, loss of income, and feelings of meaninglessness and of being alone or a burden. In the United States there is a strong negative cultural bias toward the elderly. Social isolation is real for the elderly, as is their lessened role in society and the accompanying reduction in status. The interaction of these factors leads many to deep depression, hopelessness, and suicide.

Middle-aged adults. The suicide rate per 100,000 population for white male adults between the ages of 35 and 64 years was 24.5 in 1980. Black males in the same age range had a rate of 13.1 per 100,000 population. For the same year and age range, white females had a suicide rate of 9.5 per 100,000 and black females a rate of 3.2 per 100,000.[23]

The short-term trend for middle-aged adults was in a pattern of flux when viewed across several years. In 1983 a 16.4 suicide rate per 100,000 was recorded for the 35-to-64 age group. In 1986 the rate of suicide was 16.5, followed by 16.1 in 1987.[24]

The contributing factors to suicide in this age range are numerous. Occupational stresses, family needs and problems (including divorce), caring for and supporting progeny, changing self-perceptions and identity crises, various feelings of failure, alienation, normlessness, and hopelessness—the list goes on and on.

Teenagers and young adults. The increase in suicide among the young is perhaps the most startling. The suicide rate for persons between the ages of 15 and 24 years peaked in 1977 at 13.3 per 100,000 population.[25] Since that time the rates have fluctuated as noted below:

Year	Rate
1977	13.3
1978	12.1

1979	12.4
1980	12.3
1981	11.1
1982	12.2
1983	11.9
1984	12.5
1985	12.2
1986	13.1

The pattern of at-risk groups on the variables of sex and race for the 15-to-24-year age group is much the same as with older groups, with white males being most at risk, followed by black males, and with white females and black females being the least at risk. The one exception to this pattern was in 1972, when the rates for black males and females sharply increased, exceeding the rates for white males and females, respectively, for that year only, before reverting to the normal pattern.

The incidence of adolescent suicides shows a sharp increase over the last generation. The rate has tripled for young people between the ages of 10 and 19 since the late 1950s and has doubled for teens in the 15-to-19-year-old group since the late 1960s. Suicide is the third leading cause of death in the 15-to-19-year-old group, after accidents and cancer. It is the second leading cause of death among college students.[26]

Feelings of helplessness and hopelessness shaped by the struggle to become independent and deal with a complex world are major factors in teen suicides and suicide attempts (the attempts are estimated to be approximately half a million each year). Loneliness, impulsivity, confusion of identity, socioeconomic conditions, stress in the home, and peer pressure are also factors in teen suicides.[27]

Children. The U.S. Department of Health and Human Services notes that "reports of suicide among very young children are rare, but suicidal behavior is not."[28] Although rough estimates are as close as anyone can come to a statistical representation of suicide among children, it is believed that "as many as 12,000 children, ages 5–14, may be hospitalized in this country every year for deliberate self-destructive acts, such as stabbing, cutting, scalding, burning, overdosing, and jumping from high places."[29] There is little doubt that the reasons for this kind of behavior are variously connected to the needs, problems, pressures, and issues that children face in home, school, peer group, and community life.

Sex

Males. In all age groups, most completed suicides are committed by males. Males also use the most lethal methods to kill themselves; 64.3 percent used firearms in 1981 as compared with 40.7 percent of completed female suicides, and the figures for 1985 are not appreciably different, with 64 percent of all suicides by males having been committed by the use of firearms and 40.5 percent of all suicides committed by females.[30] Whereas in 1982 76.6 percent of all recorded suicides were committed by males, the percentage had increased to 78.6 percent by 1985.[31]

Females. In 1984 the suicide rate for females was 5.4 per 100,000 population, as compared to 19.7 for males. This translates to 6,597 deaths by suicide for women in 1984 as compared to 22,689 for men.[32] In 1985 there was a slight decline in the number of women committing suicide, to 6,308, or 21.4 percent of all suicides for that year.[33] Four times more women than men attempt suicide. Women tend to use less lethal means, although this is gradually changing; one third of females 25 years old and up used guns to commit suicide, but over one half of females in the 15-to-24-year range used guns, according to U.S. Department of Health and Human Services statistics.[34]

Race

The suicide rate per 100,000 for blacks in 1984 was 6.2, as compared to the rate of 13.4 for whites. Sharp increases in the suicide rate can be observed for black males in recent years, with rates for black males in some urban areas reported to exceed white males in the same age group.[35] Suicide rates peak among black males in their early twenties and have been increasing. "Although black males made up 1 percent of the population between the ages of 25 and 34, in 1980 they represented 17.8 percent of 25-to-29-year-old suicide victims, and 14.3 percent of those between 30 and 34 years old."[36] The rate of suicide per 100,000 for black males in the 25-to-34 age group was 19.6 in 1985, the highest rate of any of the age groups from 10 to 85 years and over. Black females in the same age group showed a rate of 3 per 100,000.[37] The most telling figures are those for black females, which continue to show them to be the lowest at-risk group.

Marital Status

Among those who live alone, the widowed, divorced, and separated are at higher risk for suicide. It is important to distinguish between the widowed, divorced, and separated who live alone and those who live with others. Yet statistical data show that "because more adults are married, more adult suicides are married."[38] The underlying implication is that a healthy relationship with others reduces the incidence of loneliness and despair and, at the same time, the tendency to commit suicide.

A Sociotheological View:
What Can the Churches Do and How?

The prevailing cultural bias in America generally opposes suicide. The primary underlying assumption that shapes our religious culture, our beliefs, and our moral stance maintains that suicide is wrong and cannot be justified through the eyes of faith. Suicide is not to be committed by the believer and is to be prevented from happening regardless of the circumstances. Despite devastating situations of suffering, meaninglessness, deprivation, and oppression where suicide would be considered a justifiable option by some, it is generally rejected and deemed inappropriate by the churches and viewed as a serious problem in the society.

The particular experiences of some people who appear more likely to respond with suicidal behavior would suggest that many believe there are greater goods and greater evils than suicide among life's choices. Although considerable theological and ethical rethinking is being directed to the problem of suicide and the right to end one's own life with dignity,[39] the remainder of this discussion will operate from the prevailing value scheme, which deems suicide to be tragically wrong and a behavioral response that should be prevented.

A crucial bit of information for this concluding section is drawn from the finding in the sociological study of religion that, in cultures where the suicide taboo has been established, religion helps to prevent suicide, partly because of its function as a social integrator and partly because of its religious content. This can be illustrated by referring to the religions of Africa and to western Christianity. The churches, then, would be well advised to take seriously their own religious message and consciously develop modes of response (ministries) that demonstrate its decisive significance. The proliferation of denominations and the number of congregations notwithstanding, the churches have two foundational elements upon which to build, the organized community of the faithful itself and the radically implemented Christian faith message of justice, hope, and peace.

If indeed participatory social action can be anticipated in addressing the "problem" of suicide, a realistic assessment of available resources is imperative. The religious group or community itself is, ideally, a primary resource. To the extent that the churches' social organization and religious message are effectively administered and projected, they have the power to offer alternatives to suicide for individuals, the culture, and society.

In the American social context the value of human life is seriously diminished by homicides and suicides that are so frequent as to become commonplace and accepted as inevitable responses to crisis and conflict. The patterns of drug trafficking and abuse provide a vivid illustration of homicidal and suicidal behaviors.

One of the profound problems is that there is no social institution or group of institutions working to stem the tide of suicides effectively. Various messages, therapies, and interventions are available, but they produce minimal results for the disproportionately at-risk groups—teenagers, young adult black males, elderly white males, and the elderly in general.

There is an operative double standard in the culture relative to the value of human life: the darker the skin hue, the more extreme the age limits (very young or very old), and the lower the social, political, and economic position, the greater is society's tolerance of acts of destruction of human life. The result is a dulling of the senses concerning the redemptive possibilities for life together in human community.

What can the church do as it faces culture and society? It can work through its various denominations and congregations to create open, receptive communities. These communities need to understand themselves and act as part of a network to provide nurturing, caring, supporting ministries that transform, enable, and encourage persons from within for the missional activity of reaching out and caring. The congregations become centers for refuge and relief but also participant groups in the work of identifying and proclaiming the new possibilities and advocating and resourcing church-based and community-based ministries for those suicidally at risk or potentially at risk. None of this is possible if the churches, as the People of God, do not believe and take seriously the religious message of the Christian faith.

Another important presumption is that intervention and planned social action can produce social change—change toward responses that are valued in church and community as compared with those that are disvalued. Not only can there be change in individual orientations to action, there must also be change in the social structures and processes that invariably influence tendencies toward suicide, on the one hand, and the struggle to survive and cope, on the other. The presumption that intervention, therapy, and social action can make a difference is held by other caregivers and their respective agencies. Whether or not these other agencies or social institutions can indeed make a difference depends, theoretically, on their social integrative function and their functional religious content (that is, their beliefs, rituals, interpretative myth or story, and their external or transcendent referent). If the total effort of alternative caregivers is devoted to individual therapy exclusive of social therapy and social change, the likelihood of preventing suicide attempts and reducing the suicide rate is no better than in the case of a lopsided, deficient religious response from the churches.

The church must respond out of the recognition that there are social reasons for increased suicides just as there are social ways to reduce suicides. If, on the one hand, listening, counseling, and providing meaning, guidance, and support are important modes of action directed to individuals, those responses have counterparts that should be directed to the society and its systems. Listening to the society to hear the calls for help and discern the clues of despair is no less important than listening to individuals. Value formation and norm-building for individual characters have counterparts in the society. Advocacy and action to transform individual lives are also necessary for the transformation of the larger social group.

One of the most compelling purposes of the Christian churches is that of participating in God's mission and ministry of transforming the world. It is everywhere apparent that faithfulness to the missional task requires, among other things, concrete action in the realm of the social. The expanding issue of suicide requires listening, becoming aware, and providing informed, nurturing socialization and integration of persons and groups, support for those who face life-threatening crises and developmental processes, and far-reaching efforts for social change. In the absence of faithful response by the churches and other institutions, suicide rates will continue to increase, to the detriment of the whole of society.

NOTES

1. Émile Durkheim, *Suicide: A Study in Sociology,* tr. John A. Spaulding and George Simpson (New York: Free Press, 1951).

2. Black sociologist and social ethicist C. Eric Lincoln is perhaps foremost among those developing theories based on the experiences of specific minority and majority groups in contemporary society. See, for example, his book *Race, Reli-*

gion, and the Continuing American Dilemma (New York: Hill & Wang, 1984) for a probing analysis of the experiences of black people.

3. Ibid., p. 42.

4. Ibid., p. 43.

5. Mark Betley in *Issue Pak: Understanding Teenage Suicide, a Gatekeeper's Approach,* ed. Dorothy Jeffcoat (Lutheran Church in America, Division for Parish Services), p. 8. This is one of the few church publications to provide a well-researched discussion of the question of suicide among teenagers.

6. See *DOA/Cause of Death: Suicide,* produced by the U.S. Department of Health and Human Services and the National Institute of Mental Health (Washington, D.C.: U.S. Government Printing Office, 1986); publications by the American Association of Suicidology; and Betley, *Issue Pak: Understanding Teenage Suicide,* p. 4.

7. Durkheim, *Suicide,* pp. 46–52.

8. Ibid., p. 276.

9. Ibid., pp. 208–209.

10. William Sims Bainbridge and Rodney Stark, "Suicide, Homicide, and Religion: Durkheim Reassessed," *Annual Review of the Social Sciences of Religion* 5:53 (1981).

11. See Durkheim, *Suicide,* p. 51.

12. Rodney Stark, Daniel P. Doyle, and Jesse Lynn Rushing, "Beyond Durkheim: Religion and Suicide," *Journal for the Scientific Study of Religion* 22(2):120 (1983).

13. Ibid., p. 121.

14. Émile Durkheim, *The Elementary Forms of Religious Life,* tr. Joseph Ward Swain (New York: Free Press, 1965), p. 62.

15. Stark, Doyle, and Rushing, "Beyond Durkheim," p. 123.

16. Ibid., p. 129.

17. K. D. Breault, "Suicide in America: A Test of Durkheim's Theory of Religious and Family Integration, 1933–1980," *American Journal of Sociology* 92(3):632 (Nov. 1986).

18. Bainbridge and Stark, "Suicide, Homicide, and Religion," p. 53.

19. James T. Clemons, "Suicide: A Neglected Issue," *Engage/Social Action,* April 1985, pp. 26 and 27.

20. In John L. McIntosh, "Elderly Suicide" (unpublished

paper), September 24, 1986; and Nancy J. Osgood, "Suicide in the Elderly: Are We Heeding the Warnings?" *Postgraduate Medicine: The Journal of Applied Medicine for the Primary Care Physician* 72(2):123–130 (1982).

21. See U.S. Bureau of the Census, *Statistical Abstract of the United States, 1988* (Washington, D.C.: U.S. Government Printing Office, 1987), p. 17, table 20. Also see provisional data from the National Center for Health Statistics, "Annual Summary of Births, Marriages, Divorces, and Deaths: United States, 1987," *Monthly Vital Statistics Report* 36(13):19 (July 29, 1988).

22. *Statistical Abstract of the United States, 1988,* p. 15, table 16. Note that the 12.2 percent figure is derived from the combined total of those 65 years of age and older in relationship to the projected total U.S. population for 1987. The 1987 provisional data on suicides is derived from *Monthly Vital Statistics Report,* cited in note 21.

23. The suicide rates were calculated from "Suicide Rates by Sex, Race, and Age Groups: 1970–1981," in *Statistical Abstract of the United States, 1985,* p. 79, table 118.

24. See National Center for Health Statistics, "Annual Summary of Births, Deaths, Marriages, and Divorces: United States, 1983," *Monthly Vital Statistics Report* 32(13):18 (Sept. 21, 1984); also 36(13):19 (July 29, 1988) (cited in note 21).

25. See Centers for Disease Control, *Youth Suicide Surveillance, Summary: 1970–1980* (Washington, D.C.: U.S. Government Printing Office, 1986), pp. 13 and 16. Also see *Monthly Vital Statistics Report* 32(13):18 (cited in note 24) and 34(13):20 (September 19, 1986).

26. Arthur S. Freese, "Adolescent Suicide: Mental Health Challenge," Public Affairs Pamphlet No. 569 (Public Affairs Committee, April 1984).

27. Ibid., p. 8.

28. *DOA/Cause of Death: Suicide* (cited in note 6), p. 4.

29. Ibid.

30. *Statistical Abstract of the United States, 1985,* p. 79, table 118; see also *Statistical Abstract of the United States, 1988,* p. 82, table 125.

31. Information on the increasing percentage of male sui-

cides between the years 1982 and 1985 was extracted from *Statistical Abstract of the United States, 1988,* p. 82, table 125.

32. John L. McIntosh, "U.S. Suicide in 1984" (unpublished paper), p. 1.

33. *Statistical Abstract of the United States, 1988,* p. 82.

34. *DOA/Cause of Death: Suicide* (cited in note 6), p. 5.

35. *DOA/Cause of Death: Suicide,* p. 5.

36. Lloyd Gite, "Black Men and Suicide," *Essence* magazine, November 1986, p. 64.

37. *Statistical Abstract of the United States, 1988,* p. 82, table 124.

38. *DOA/Cause of Death: Suicide* (cited in note 6), p. 5.

39. See *Suicide and the Right to Die,* ed. by Jacques Pohier and Dietmar Mieth, *Concilium: Religion in the Eighties* 179 (Edinburgh: T. & T. Clark, 1985), especially "Ethical Arguments in Favor of Suicide" by Annemarie Pieper, "Associations for the Right to Die in Dignity" by Paula Caucanas-Pisier, "Life No Longer Has Any Meaning for Me" by Jean-Pierre Jossua, "A Right to a Freely Chosen Death? Some Theological Considerations" by Adrian Holderegger, and "Have Christians the Right to Kill Themselves? From Self-Murder to Self-Killing" by Harry Kuitert.

3

Biblical Perspectives
James T. Clemons

JAMES T. CLEMONS is Professor of New Testament at Wesley Theological Seminary, where he has taught since 1967. In the mid-60s he was chaplain to Morningside College in Sioux City, Iowa, and, earlier, field representative for Hendrix College in Conway, Arkansas, his alma mater. He holds the B.D. degree from Perkins School of Theology and the Ph.D. in Biblical Studies from Duke University and is an ordained elder in The United Methodist Church.

Clemons's interest in suicide grew out of his teaching and biblical studies and was stimulated by social and pastoral concerns. He has conducted workshops and lectured in nine states and has written and edited several articles and two other books on the subject.

There are three basic reasons why a biblical perspective is necessary for a clear understanding of suicide in America today. First, it has been used to justify religious dogma. Since the time of Augustine in the fourth century C.E., the church has insisted that suicide is a sin—at times, an unforgivable one. Much of the church's failure to respond theologically and pastorally to the current crisis comes from the centuries-old insistence on the inherent evils of suicide in virtually all its forms.

Second, the Bible has been used by the church to influence societies to look upon suicide not only as a sin but also as a crime. Many of the laws about suicide, particularly in Western nations, came about as the result of societal attitudes shaped by the church. This fact is even more pronounced in countries like the United States, where the Bible is frequently viewed as the source of all ethical—hence, legal—wisdom. Many people believe that if the Bible says something is wrong, there ought to be a law against it.

Third, moral teachings based on the Bible affect the psychological underpinnings of countless individuals. So entrenched has been the biblically based teaching against suicide that psychotherapists and pastoral counselors often must work through layers of guilt and repressed hostility in order to help survivors cope with their problems.

Directly related to these psychological and social realities are the effects of a residual social stigma against suicide that often goes beyond any legal requirement. Public abuses against the bodies of known suicides, once seen as a way of preventing what was deemed to be a terrible sin and heinous crime, were bizarre to the point of being little more than macabre orgies. In England as late as the eighteenth century, heirs of suicides were denied the inheritance that otherwise would have been their due.

Today, much of the needless pain survivors feel because of society's lingering stigma must be laid at the doorstep of the church and the ways it has interpreted the Bible. Ironically, the problem is seen to be even more devastating as suicidologists now cite the stigma itself as a major obstacle in the prevention of suicide! This point was mentioned more than once in a series of reports from the Secretary's Task Force on Youth Suicide. With this awareness of the importance of biblical perspectives for an informed understanding of suicide in America today, we proceed to two other important aspects of the issue.

When we ask, What does the Bible say about suicide?, two types of decisions must be made before a proper answer can be given. On the one hand, we must decide how broadly or how narrowly we are going to define the term so that we can determine which biblical texts may be used as evidence. On the other hand, we must have at least a general idea of how we are going to go about interpreting whatever evidence we have chosen to examine.

Because one's method of interpreting the Bible is less frequently discussed than the texts they interpret, I discuss that subject first. Then, after some comments on definitions, I shall survey three kinds of biblical material that have been used to formulate opinions on suicide.

The Importance of Method in Interpreting the Bible

How does one go about using the Bible to make a moral judgment? The question is as old as the Bible itself, for within its pages there are many different interpretations from later writers of what had been written and accepted earlier. For example, the account of the Ten Commandments in Deuteronomy 4 comes out of a social, economic, and theological situation different from that of the original setting as recorded in Exodus 20; this difference in historical situation explains the noticeable differences in interpretation between the two accounts. Again, Paul and other New Testament writers, following a long tradition among Jewish writers, reworked several texts from Hebrew scriptures in the light of their own experience of God's revelation and different worldview. These are only two of many examples of the ways in which later generations of the faithful engaged in reinterpreting earlier writings and traditions. The process has been at work throughout biblical history.

The same appropriation of scripture in order to justify moral decisions can be seen at every stage in the history of the church and synagogue. Every important facet of life within Jewish and Christian communities has been subject to a wide range of interpretation. What the Bible says has always been used to help shape the thought and response of the faithful. Conversely, what a community experienced and believed has often been a factor in how it interpreted scripture.

Interpretation, understandably, comes in many forms. Study of the various methods—what caused them, how they developed, how they have been applied—is the proper concern of hermeneutics. Over the past decade or so, scholars have given renewed attention to the history of biblical hermeneutics in order to see how interpretations in a given period were affected by a variety of social factors. Occasionally the church has also employed practical and philosophic arguments—what is sometimes called "the world's wisdom"—to argue for specific theological, ethical, and legal positions.

The practice of reinterpreting the scriptures in the light of new experiences, with roots going back to the Bible itself, is still in evidence today. It is for this reason that each person needs to be clear on how he or she will use biblical texts to make ethical decisions.

Even those who say they believe in literal interpretation often fail to see precisely what that term means, where it originated, how it has changed its meaning, and what the implications are of adhering to it in either a rigid or somewhat flexible manner. Those who prefer a more nearly "critical" method of interpretation have the same responsibility. *How* we interpret is as important as *what* we interpret. Our hermeneutic can be used either to support what we already believe or to challenge our most deeply held convictions. Regardless of how careful, how precise, or how persuasive an exegete may be, in the final analysis it is the individual reader who must decide what the Bible says to him or to her. That decision should be based on the best insights available on what the chosen texts meant in their original setting and how the meanings have been understood at different times in history. Equally as important is an awareness of the factors that are currently influencing our interpretation, such as new medical understandings, personal experiences, and current statistics.

A Word About Definition

Strange as it may seem, even to begin a look at what the Bible says about suicide requires a clear definition of the term. Many people, in their examination of the biblical evidence, simply do not consider some rather obvious accounts of persons who chose to end their lives. This omission occurs even in some of the major biblical commentaries and dictionaries of the Bible, where suicide is often entirely overlooked.

I prefer to define the term in a very broad sense. A wide-angle approach will allow us to examine a larger number of passages before grouping them into different categories. A broad definition also provides a better perspective on what the Bible really says about the subject.

The definition I shall be using is simply this: *Suicide is the deliberate choice and successful effort to end one's life, regardless of the motives, circumstances, or methods used.* Several suicidologists have recently struggled with the problem of definition, recognizing that scientific research must be guided by definitions that are as precise as possible. Their work goes beyond the categories first laid out by Émile Durkheim in his classic sociological study published in 1897.

Two definitions were given by contributors to the 1985 volume of the Roman Catholic publication *Concilium: Religion in the Eighties.* That issue was titled *Suicide and the Right to Die,* which in itself shows how the subject is at last drawing renewed theological attention, even among Roman Catholics, whose traditional rigid stance against suicide is well known.

Niceto Blázquez, Director of the Pontifical Institute of Philosophy in Madrid, began his article with the statement, "Suicide is the act by which a person directly, knowingly, and freely brings about his or her own death." He went on to point out that moral theologians do not include those who "take their lives in a state of mental abnormality or who cannot be held responsible for their action."[1]

Along the same lines, Harry Kuitert, Professor of Ethics and Systematic Theology of the Free University in Amsterdam, used this definition:

> The simplest definition of suicide is the deliberate ending of one's own life, whatever the circumstances, intentions, or means to achieve this end may play in the process. This definition does not contain any value-judgment, but value-judgments obviously have no place in definitions.[2]

It is my broad definition that will guide the following discussion.

Examining the Biblical Evidence

Three types of biblical texts will be considered. First are passages that give direct accounts of persons who deliberately ended their lives, one way or another, and those who made the attempt to do so. Second are texts that, although they make no specific reference to suicide, have been used to condemn the act. Third are texts that have been used to condone the act, even though such texts contain no explicit reference to suicide. These indirect references refer to the meaning of life, or to human values that relate to the quality and purpose of life, or to those qualities of God and the teachings of Jesus that can be applied to the subject of suicide.

The Direct Evidence

In considering the direct accounts, we must note not just the fact that a suicide or suicide attempt occurred but how the account was recorded. Thus we shall be concerned with such questions as: What does the story tell us about the author's original purpose in including it? What attitudes toward suicide do such direct accounts reflect, and how did they help shape the community of faith at that particular time? How were early accounts treated by biblical writers of later centuries?

These questions become particularly important in the light of recent biblical scholarship, with its emphasis on redaction and rhetorical and canonical criticism. As we turn to a closer look at the direct accounts, such concerns will be basic to our searching of the scriptures, even though we cannot discuss all of them in detail.

Saul and His Armor-Bearer. The most prominent figure to commit suicide in Hebrew scripture was Saul. His long and illustrious life came to its tragic end in a battle that saw three of his sons killed, all his men lost, and Saul himself badly wounded and facing the certainly of capture, ridicule, and torture by his enemies.

In a few short verses, the author ends the story of Saul in these poignant words:

> Then Saul said to his armor-bearer, "Draw your sword, and thrust me through with it, lest these uncircumcised come and thrust me through, and make sport of me." But his armor-bearer would not; for he feared greatly. Therefore Saul took his own

sword, and fell upon it. And when his armor-bearer saw that Saul was dead, he also fell upon his sword, and died with him. Thus Saul died, and his three sons, and his armor-bearer, and all his men, on the same day together. . . .

On the morrow, when the Philistines came to strip the slain, they found Saul and his three sons fallen on Mount Gilboa. And they cut off his head, and stripped off his armor, and sent messengers throughout the land of the Philistines, to carry the good news to their idols and to the people. They put his armor in the temple of Ashtaroth; and they fastened his body to the wall of Bethshan. But when the inhabitants of Jabesh-gilead heard what the Philistines had done to Saul, all the valiant men arose, and went all night, and took the body of Saul and the bodies of his sons from the wall of Bethshan; and they came to Jabesh and burnt them there. And they took their bones and buried them under the tamarisk tree in Jabesh, and fasted seven days.

1 Samuel 31:4–6, 8–13

As we can see, the story does not end merely with Saul's death. Rather, it closes with the account of the valiant men of Jabesh-gilead, who at risk of their own lives went to retrieve Saul's body so they might treat it with reverence and respect. Then they grieved over the loss of their king.

In terms of the attitudes of the community, for whom this story became holy scripture, there is no suggestion that Saul or even his armor-bearer were in any way to be condemned for their actions.

But to get the complete picture of how Saul was remembered by the Israelites, we have also to consider several other passages. Immediately after this brief but descriptive account of Saul's suicide, a different account of his death is given to David by a young Amalekite, who claims that he himself killed Saul at Saul's request (2 Sam. 1:1–16). Upon hearing this blatant confession, David has the Amalekite killed, because he had dared "put forth [his] hand to destroy the LORD's anointed." The prevailing opinion among biblical scholars is that this fabrication is the claim of an ambitious young man, seeking to feather his own nest.

Then, as if to underscore the continuing grief of the community over Saul's death, there is in the same chapter a psalm of lament (vs. 24–25):

> Ye daughters of Israel, weep over Saul,
>   who clothed you daintily in scarlet,
>   who put ornaments of gold upon your apparel.
>
> How are the mighty fallen
>   in the midst of the battle!

David says that this lament, which he may have written himself, should be taught to all the people of Judah. Again, the clear emphasis is on the grief of David over the death of Saul and, by extension, the grief of his people, with no concern for the manner in which he died.

At a later point in 2 Samuel (2:4b–7), when David hears that the valiant men of Jabesh-gilead have buried and honored Saul, he asks for the Lord's blessing upon them for their loyalty to their former king. That is to say, those who honored and revered Saul, who died by his own hand, were in turn respected and favored by David. By so honoring those who honored Saul, David further instilled in the minds of the community the idea that there was no condemnation for those who honored a suicide.

One other account of Saul's death comes in what scholars call the Later Tradition, found in 1–2 Chronicles. Characteristic of this later account, written some three to four hundred years after 1–2 Samuel, is the clear elevation of David above Saul. The author of Chronicles seems to have used every opportunity to put Saul in an unfavorable light.

The actual account of Saul's death by his own hand in 1 Chronicles is almost identical with that given at the end of 1 Samuel. What follows, however, is not David's psalm of lament over Saul but quite the opposite, a scathing epitaph to Saul's life.

> So Saul died for his unfaithfulness; he was unfaithful to the LORD in that he did not keep the command of the LORD, and also consulted a medium, seeking guidance, and did not seek guidance from the LORD. Therefore, the LORD slew him, and turned the kingdom over to David.
>
> 1 Chronicles 10:13–14

It is of particular interest here that, in the midst of some rather harsh words about Saul, the chronicler again does not use the manner of Saul's death against him! If there had been the slightest notion that Saul had done evil by deliberately falling on his sword, the chronicler would certainly have used the incident to further his intent to put down Saul and elevate David. We must conclude that even at this much later date, suicide per se was not condemned, either by the biblical writers or by the community for whom their writings were to become holy scripture.

Unfortunately, poor Saul was not yet ready to rest in peace. In 2 Samuel 21, as part of a bizarre story involving the execution of seven of Saul's descendants, David removes the bones of Saul's body once more, taking them from Jabesh-gilead and placing them in the tomb of his father, as a final tribute to the revered king. To be sure, it could be argued that this act was yet another example of David's astute political practicality. But again, quite apart from any real or imagined political motivation, there is no concern expressed in the account to show that the manner of Saul's death was to be used either to demean his sacred memory or to condemn the practice of suicide.

There are five other direct accounts of suicide in Hebrew scriptures, each reflecting a different method and motive. These we may review much more briefly.

Ahithophel. In 2 Samuel 17:23, after his counsel for the would-be king Absalom has been rejected, it is said of Ahithophel that he "went off home to his own city . . . set his house in order, and hanged himself." The brief account ends with the simple statement that "he died, and was buried in the tomb of his father."

Zimri. In 1 Kings 16:15–20, Zimri, another would-be king, has only a few days of glory before ending his own life by setting fire to his house within the city, which is then besieged. Although Zimri reportedly died for his sins, the manner of his death is not listed among them.

Samson. A more popular figure, of course, is Samson. After a life given largely to fighting the Philistines, he spent his last years blinded and tormented by his enemies. Yet in a final act that is preceded by a prayer to God for the strength to get revenge and by the request that he might die with the Philistines, Samson succeeds in causing the house they are all in together to come crashing down upon them. His family then comes and buries him in his father's tomb (Judg. 16:28–31). This respect for Samson continued through the centuries, so that his name is included among those heroes of the faith listed by the author of the Epistle to the Hebrews.

In this account of Samson's death by choice, we have what might be considered a prime example of that supreme sacrifice so common among members of the world's military forces. While some would not consider such a death suicide, it must be included within the broad definition given at the beginning of this chapter. In terms of ethics, by the way, there is the question of whether or not such a generally accepted form of self-sacrifice for others must be approved only for those in battle.

Abimelech. The last two direct accounts of suicidal behavior in Hebrew scripture are similar; in both cases, death was likely to occur quite soon anyway, whether or not requests to have someone end their lives were granted.

The story of Abimelech's death is recorded succinctly in Judges 9:52–54.

> And Abimelech came to the tower, and fought against it, and drew near to the door of the tower to burn it with fire. And a certain woman threw an upper millstone upon Abimelech's head, and crushed his skull. Then he called hastily to the young man his armor-bearer, and said to him, "Draw your sword and kill me, lest men say of me, 'A woman killed him.' " And his young man thrust him through, and he died.

Apart from its almost laughable machismo, this act also must be considered a suicide by our earlier definition. Although the account goes on to state that God thus requited Abimelech for his sins, there is nothing to suggest that the divine retribution was related to the suicide itself. Suicide is neither the cause nor the form of Abimelech's punishment.

If the author, in addition to being convinced that Abimelech was sinful, had thought suicide was a terrible sin, it would have been easy for him to tie the two ideas together, as if to say, Suicide is the kind of act you would expect of such an evil person, or at least the kind of punishment such an evil person deserves. In the absence of any such statement, we can only conclude that the manner of Abimelech's death was of no serious consequence to the writer, who was only giving the facts of the case to his readers. Actually, the writer implies that to die at the hand of a woman is far worse than ordering someone else to kill you. It was a sexist attitude, not a condemnation of suicide, that this story perpetuated within the faithful community.

Jonah. The request for death by the hand of another has yet another parallel, that of Jonah. Jonah is not usually thought of as one who attempted suicide, but the account deserves our serious consideration. In the midst of a raging storm at sea, Jonah was confronted by sailors who asked, "What shall we do to you, that the sea may quiet down for us?" (1:11). Jonah's reply has strong similarities to the psychological state of many suicides and attempted suicides today: "Take me up and throw me into the sea; then the sea will quiet down for you; for I know it is because of me that this great tempest has come upon you" (Jonah 1:12).

After first trying to save themselves by greater human effort, the seamen at last decide they should do what Jonah has asked. For very practical reasons (the safety of the crew and ship), tinged with religious overtones (seen in their prayers for forgiveness for taking another's life), the men comply with Jonah's request.

We cannot, of course, be entirely sure what Jonah's motives were. He could have been purely altruistic, wanting only to save the crew, even at the cost of his own life. Or he could have been completely at his wits' end in wrestling with God, as several of his other words in this passage and at the end of the story strongly suggest. Yet having done what he thought would result in his death, Jonah, the would-be suicide, goes on to become the person through whom the wicked city of Nineveh is saved and, perhaps more importantly for the author's theology, the one through whom a significant facet of God's nature is revealed. Instead of being condemned for suicidal behavior,

Jonah comes to be considered a saint, as he is sometimes depicted in icons and illuminations.

Judas. The New Testament contains only one example of a direct account of suicide, that of Judas. Only Matthew of the Four Gospels makes any reference to Judas's death by his own hand (27:3–5). The author refers to Judas as the betrayer of Jesus, but in spite of this condemnation the statement that Judas hanged himself must be read simply as a statement of fact. To insist that suicide is bad because the betrayer of Jesus died in this way is to read into Matthew's story an attitude that did not become basic Christian teaching until the time of Augustine, some three hundred years later.

Another account of Judas's death is given in Acts 1:15–19, where there is no reference to hanging but only to the fact that Judas fell headlong and his abdomen burst open—once more, a horrible death, but no indication that the fall was a suicidal act and no explicit comment that such a death was a punishment for his betrayal of Jesus.

The book of Acts also records the attempt of the Philippian jailer to take his own life when he thinks that Paul and the other prisoners have escaped (16:25–34). Paul prevents this from happening by shouting out in the nick of time that all the guard's prisoners are still there. Some would see this as an example for Christians to prevent all forms of suicide. Others would read the passage only as Paul's preventing a needless death based on false assumptions. Still others would see it primarily as an example of the way in which Paul was an effective evangelist even in the least fortuitous circumstances, which was part of the overall purpose of the author of Acts. Neither here nor anywhere in Paul's several vice lists does he condemn the act of suicide as a sin.

In view of this rather large amount of biblical evidence related directly to suicide, plus the even larger amount of indirect evidence to be discussed next, we certainly would not expect to find so little discussion of the subject in otherwise first-rate encyclopedias and dictionaries of the Bible, several of which make no reference to it whatever. Some of the leading commentaries hardly touch the subject or its implications when giving an exegesis of the accounts just discussed, and general works on related subjects make only passing references to suicide, even though it was obviously a well-known form of death throughout biblical times. A few of the older works show a quite narrow bias against suicide, which simply does not do justice to the standards of historical critical exegesis.

Students of the Bible who are accustomed to relying on such aids for understanding and guidance are thus forewarned not to expect the help on suicide they could reasonably expect when researching other topics in standard reference works.

This concludes the brief survey of Bible passages in which direct accounts of suicide or attempted suicide occur. It shows that the deliberate choice to end one's life was well known over several centuries and in several types of literature. A variety of methods, circumstances, and motives were recorded. Yet this part of the evidence for a biblical perspective offers no basis for the kind of outright condemnation that came to be the church's official position in later centuries.

The Indirect Evidence

The second type of biblical evidence is found in texts that have been used to condemn suicide, even though the texts themselves do not refer directly to this act. A look at these is important for an understanding of suicide today, for they have been part of the means whereby the church has helped to shape attitudes in Western nations for at least fifteen hundred years.

Here we must observe two words of caution. First, we must be quite selective in listing the examples, for the total number of examples so used is surprisingly large. Second, we must exercise great care in identifying indirect references that condemn or condone suicide, for one always runs the danger of reading into a particular passage (eisegesis) a point of view one already holds, whether or not the text actually intended that meaning.

As we have seen, this has often been the case with the account of Judas's death. The biblical story in and of itself does not judge the manner of his death, yet that direct account has often been used to condemn the act.

In citing the following passages, therefore, I am not giving the results of my own exegesis. Rather, I am simply identifying passages that have been used, both by individuals and church councils across the centuries and by persons and groups today, to justify dogma to shape attitudes in society and to satisfy their own minds on the subject. Obviously, some of the conclusions are farfetched, but our purpose is to see more clearly the ways in which the Bible has been and is being used and where further interpretation is needed.

Condemnation. First are texts that affirm the fact that life is a gift from God, the Creator and Ruler of the universe, who alone has the power to give life and take it away and whose will is not to be contradicted or even questioned. There are also texts that set an example for the endurance of suffering in this life. Taken together, they illustrate the biblical condemnation of suicide as a sin.

Exodus 20:13, the Sixth Commandment (fifth in Roman Catholic versions), is one of the most frequently cited: "You shall not kill." It was interpreted by Augustine and others after him to include self-killing.

Deuteronomy 30:19—although it is addressed to the people of Israel and is in a passage in which the meaning of "choosing life" has nothing to do with suicide—is also used in this way. "I call heaven and earth to witness against you this day, that I have set before you life and death, blessing and curse; therefore choose life, that you and your descendants may live."

Deuteronomy 32:39 was used by Thomas Aquinas in the thirteenth century to argue against the sin of suicide because God said, "*I* kill and *I* make alive"—the choice being God's prerogative, never that of a human being.

Job 1:21 is cited by the *Interpreter's Dictionary of the Bible* (IV, 454) as being among those passages implying a prohibition against suicide: "the LORD gave and the LORD has taken away; blessed be the name of the LORD." Job's steadfast character in refusing to heed his wife's plea to "curse God and die!" is also used to show that suicide is to be rejected, even in the midst of life's most difficult circumstances.

From Paul, several passages could easily suggest that suicide is beyond the consideration of a Christian. First Corinthians 6:19 is among the most familiar: "Do you not know that your body is a temple of the Holy Spirit within you, which you have from God?" Others include Ephesians 5:29—"For no man ever hates his own flesh, but nourishes and cherishes it, as Christ does the church"—and Philippians 4:11: "Not that I complain of want; for I have learned, in whatever state I am, to be content." This verse reminds us of Job, hanging on to life no matter how adverse its conditions.

Second Corinthians 12:8–10 likewise encourages stead-fastness:

> Three times I besought the Lord about this, that it should leave me; but he said to me, "My grace is sufficient for you, for my power is made perfect in weakness." I will all the more gladly boast of my weaknesses, that the power of Christ may rest upon me. For the sake of Christ, then, I am content with weaknesses, insults, hardships, persecutions, and calamities; for when I am weak, then I am strong.

Similar to this is Romans 8:26—"Likewise the Spirit helps us in our weakness"—and another example comes from Revelation 2:10:

> Do not fear what you are about to suffer. Behold, the devil is about to throw some of you into prison, that you may be tested, and for ten days you will have tribulation. Be faithful unto death, and I will give you the crown of life.

It is easy to see how such texts could be used by faithful readers to conclude that suicide is wrong, even without the benefit of a keen theological mind or any official dogma that had been worked out in church councils.

Support. Many passages from both Hebrew and Christian scriptures can be used to support the opposite position regarding suicide. Self-chosen death has at times been seen as an option for persons of Jewish or Christian faith, but always under carefully prescribed circumstances. These have at times included cases related to devotion to military duty, the honor of God, giving one's life to save another, unbearable physical pain, and the avoidance of rape or personal disgrace.

There is also to be considered the relationship between suicide and martyrdom. Although some would see a distinct difference between the two—as is often the case—a broad definition of suicide (which here includes the direct choice to end one's life *for whatever reason*) cannot exclude martyrdom. A further reason for relating the two is the historical and psychological evidence indicating that martyrs for a cause may have at least as much personal investment at stake as they do in the cause for which they have ostensibly committed themselves. In the post-Augustinian age, for example, the church removed from its list of martyrs many of those who had killed themselves. Military records of heroic deaths occasionally, at least, include questions about the reasons for action "above and beyond the call of duty." These statements are in no way to be taken as an indictment against the noble forms of altruism that remain a constant source of the best in devotion to ideals. They do suggest that carefully made choices are a far cry from the decision to end one's life for less worthy motives.

Suicide is certainly no longer advocated as a normal course of pious action, as it was by some heretical Christian groups in the early centuries.

Psalm 139:8 suggests that regardless of where people might go, or for what reason, they have the comfort of knowing that God will be with them: "If I ascend to heaven, thou are there! If I make my bed in Sheol, thou art there!"

The Gospel of Mark can be depicted as a call to martyrdom. Several texts therein suggest that, just as Jesus' death was a deliberate form of self-sacrifice, so also should be the deaths of his followers. "If any man would come after me, let him deny himself and take up his cross and follow me. For whoever would save his life will lose it; and whoever loses his life for my sake and the gospel's will save it" (Mark 8:34–35). An interesting point here is that in Luke's Gospel, one of the parallels to this word of Jesus reads, "Let him . . . take up his cross *daily*" (9:23, emphasis added). This change reflects an emphasis on a Christianity that is to be around for a while, one of the many subtle differences between the two Gospels pointed out by redaction critics.

Throughout Mark the emphasis is far more on the actual giving of one's life in martyrdom, following the example of Jesus himself. Mark 10:45 records Jesus as saying, "For the Son of man also came not to be served but to serve, and to give his life as a ransom for many."

Perhaps the clearest calls to follow Jesus unto death come in the Johannine literature. John 13:37 records Peter as saying, "Lord . . . I will lay down my life for you." In 15:12–14, Jesus says, "This is my commandment, that you love one another as I have loved you. Greater love has no man than this, that a man lay down his life for his friends. You are my friends if you do what I command you."

First John 3:16, among several other passages from the Johannine epistles, offers a similar view: "By this we know love, that he laid down his life for us; and we ought to lay down our lives for the brethren." Another form of assurance is in 1 John 1:5–7, which includes the sentence, "the blood of Jesus . . . cleanses us from all sin."

In Acts 20:24, Paul says, "I do not account my life of any value nor as precious to myself, if only I may accomplish my course and the ministry which I have received from the Lord Jesus, to testify to the gospel of the grace of God."

Several passages from Paul's epistles have been used to give support to suicide. Romans 5:7 affirms, "Why, one will hardly die for a righteous man—though perhaps for a good man one will dare even to die."

Romans 8:37–39 reveals Paul's own unshakable faith "that neither death, nor life, nor angels, nor principalities, nor things present, nor things to come, nor powers, nor height, nor depth, nor anything in all creation, will be able to separate us from the love of God in Christ Jesus our Lord." Note again the similarities to the assurance found in Psalm 139 and 1 John 1:5–7.

Romans 14:7–8 is in some ways even more explicit. "None of us lives to himself, and none of us dies to himself. If we live, we live to the Lord, and if we die, we die to the Lord; so then, whether we live or whether we die, we are the Lord's." Here there is no condition placed on the manner of one's death.

Second Corinthians 5:1 offers this thought, without any conditions attached: "For we know that if the earthly tent we live in is destroyed, we have a building from God, a house not made with hands, eternal in the heavens."

A final example comes from Philippians 1:21–23:

> For me to live is Christ, and to die is gain. If it is to be life in the flesh, that means fruitful labor for me. Yet which I shall choose I cannot tell. I am hard pressed between the two. My desire is to depart and be with Christ, for that is far better.

Paul's decision was to remain in the flesh, in order to be of service to others. Yet he did not consider desiring "to be with Christ," or even weighing that decision, to be wrong.

Summary

In considering the texts that have been used to shape opinions about suicide, either for it or against it, we must bear in mind that biblical texts alone do not have the final answer to so complex a problem. The direct accounts do not condemn suicide outright, and the indirect evidence has been subject to a wide variety of interpretation. An informed and effective response to the suicide crisis in America today must be based on several perspectives.

Yet biblical texts have been and still are very important in shaping the attitudes of individuals and religious communities. They still influence voters, lawmakers, judges, and jury members. Thus biblical interpretation continues to play a major role in the way ethical decisions are made and how people in difficulty attempt to cope with their personal problems. A look at the biblical evidence is an appropriate place for all persons concerned about suicide to begin their reflections on how to respond to the tremendous challenge that this current national tragedy forces upon us. But it is not the only place people should look before deciding on their own response.

NOTES

1. Niceto Blázquez, O.P., "The Church's Traditional Moral Teaching on Suicide," *Suicide and the Right to Die,* ed. by Jacques Pohier and Dietmar Mieth, *Concilium: Religion in the Eighties* 179 (Edinburgh: T. & T. Clark, 1985), p. 63.

2. Harry Kuitert, "Have Christians the Right to Kill Themselves? From Self-Murder to Self-Killing," *Suicide and the Right to Die,* p. 103.

4

Ethical Perspectives in Review

Dana W. Wilbanks

DANA W. WILBANKS is Professor of Christian Ethics at The Iliff School of Theology in Denver, Colorado. He received his B.A. from Trinity University, his M.Div. from Union Theological Seminary in New York, and his Ph.D. from Duke University. He is co-author of *Decision Making and the Bible* with H. Edward Everding and co-editor of *The Peacemaking Struggle: Militarism and Resistance* with Ronald H. Stone and has written and lectured on topics of Christian ethics and international relations, the peacemaking responsibility of the church, and biomedical ethics. His chief academic interest is the relation of Christian ethics and public policy questions, and his teaching frequently involves an interdisciplinary and interprofessional approach to these issues.

Wilbanks currently serves as chair of the Religion and Social Change Area of the joint Ph.D. program at the University of Denver and The Iliff School of Theology. He is an ordained minister of the Presbyterian Church (U.S.A.) and serves on the social policy formation committee of the General Assembly of the Presbyterian Church.

Suicide is one human action that touches particularly deep levels of feeling and belief. In the history of Christian ethics, the moral response has generally been exceedingly negative. Today this moral tradition is no longer convincing for increasing numbers of persons, though residues of its influence may continue to affect their reactions.

An investigation into contemporary Christian ethical reflection on suicide provides two dominant impressions. First is a growing appreciation for the complexity of the topic. The second is the shifting character of Christian thought about suicide.

The Complexity of Suicide

The difficulties involved in approaching suicide ethically can readily be seen. The suicide of an old person suffering from an incurable illness is different from the suicide of a despairing young adult who is spouse and parent and in reasonably good physical health. The suicide of a political prisoner to keep from betraying other persons while being tortured is different from the suicide of a lonely and painfully afflicted teenager. Certainly an ethical evaluation depends a great deal on circumstances and context. The worth of general moral judgment seems highly questionable.

Some persons even doubt that it is appropriate to deal with suicide in terms of right and wrong. Do those who commit suicide choose to do so, or are they so driven by forces beyond their control that it is an error to speak of it as their decision? Some persons might readily affirm that suicide is usually tragic and terribly sad but wonder what difference it makes whether it is judged right or wrong. A moral judgment does not help the person who committed suicide, and it may be more harmful than helpful to loved ones trying to cope with the act and the loss. Why even bring ethics into the picture? Suicide to such persons is a pastoral care issue, not an ethical one.

Yet many persons who have studied suicide regard it as often a rational and moral choice: the person consciously chooses suicide and does so for reasons he or she believes not only make it necessary but even right. Certainly among persons who choose suicide there are wide gradations of rationality. Some suicides may indeed be rooted in mental illness; many are not. Even though persons may believe suicide is the only option for coping with an unbearable life, it nonetheless is a choice based on reasons that are compelling to them.[1]

Even the definition of suicide evokes considerable discussion and debate. What kinds of acts are included: martyrdom; refusing lifesaving therapy; direct, voluntary euthanasia?[2] Most persons seem to agree that, whatever the reason, suicide is best defined in terms of the person's *intention.* Did the person intend his or her death by the action or inaction? Glenn Graber defines suicide "as doing something that results in one's death in the way that was planned, either from the intention of ending one's life or the intention to bring about some other state of affairs (such as relief from pain) that one thinks it certain or highly probable can be achieved only by means of death."[3] This definition is intended to include most instances that persons are likely to refer to as suicides in ordinary language but would exclude those acts which end in death but were intended as a desperate cry for help. The act whereby a person takes a fatal dose of drugs yet leaves a note saying she or he does not want to die is not suicide but accidental death.

Thus there is a great deal of complexity about the ethics of suicide: whether it is an ethical question, under what circumstances it occurs, what kinds of acts are involved, what the motivations are. Certainly, to make a sweeping moral condemnation of suicide (as many persons have been taught) is not helpful.

The Shifting Character of Ethical Reflection

This points to the second impression: namely, the shifting character of ethical and religious reflection on suicide. In the not too far distant past one encountered a virtually unassailable dogma that suicide was not only immoral but an especially reprehensible—maybe even unforgivable—sin. What has changed to make persons far less certain about this judgment?

With the advent of sophisticated medical technologies that can prolong life or death, it is very difficult now to believe that God determines the timing of a person's death. In contemporary medical practice it is simply all too clear that human decisions have a great deal to do with when and how one dies. It is not surprising, therefore, that the option of suicide is considered very differently from the way it was when dying was seen as a natural or providential occurrence.

An additional reason for shifting attitudes, at least in our society, is the spread of psychological understandings of human behavior. Although this does not necessarily lead to moral approval of suicide, it does mean that persons are much less likely to condemn it and much more likely to search for the factors that help us understand it. Many people, including people of religious faith, are now inclined to deal with suicide as a psychological issue rather than an ethical one.

A further reason may be found in the increasing emphasis on the rights of individuals to make their own decisions about life and death. Even though few would regard this as an absolute, the principle of personal self-determination has become more and more important and maybe even dominant in biomedical ethics. For example, whether or not to have an abortion is increasingly regarded as a question to be answered by the pregnant woman. Similarly, many people believe hospital patients should have a Bill of Rights to protect them from medical paternalism. Most agree that persons have the right to determine for themselves whether they will submit to experimental procedures or even basic treatments.

This emphasis on personal autonomy and the right of self-determination is by no means new. It is rooted in the liberal, individualistic philosophies of the West. But it has become more influential in recent years, and many more people today, including people of religious faith, speak about the right to suicide as an expression of one's right to self-determination in conditions in which living becomes intolerable.

The play *Whose Life Is It Anyway?* and the subsequent movie reveal this changing attitude. The drama is about a quadriplegic who wants to die but needs assistance. Instead, the doctor treats him for depression and regards a request to die as inherently irrational and immoral. Several years ago, I had the experience of viewing the play several times. The audiences reacted with real hostility to the doctor and with strong support for the patient and his right to die. Although this response is clearly what the author intended, the audience reaction nonetheless emphasizes the increasing level of popular support for the principle of self-determination, even when this involves the right to suicide in debilitating circumstances

Traditional Judgments About Suicide

Obvious cultural changes have helped bring about shifting attitudes toward suicide. But churches have been slow to reflect on these changes and to struggle anew with how their theologies and ethics bear on the matter. Precisely because of shifting views, this is an important and opportune time to rethink the various issues.

The first task in such rethinking is to understand and examine critically the church's traditionally negative judgments about suicide. In a recent article, James Clemons quotes John Wesley:

> It is a melancholy consideration, that there is no country in Europe, or perhaps in the habitable world, where the horrid crime of self-murder is so common as it is in England! . . . But how can this vile abuse of the law be prevented, and this execrable crime effectually discouraged? By a very easy method. We read in ancient history, that, at a certain period, many of the women of Sparta murdered themselves. This fury increasing, a law was made, that the body of every woman that killed herself should be exposed naked in the streets. The fury ceased at once. Only let a law be made and rigorously executed, that the body of every self-murderer, Lord or peasant, shall be hanged in chains, and the English fury will cease at once.[4]

This quote points both to the moral revulsion with which suicide has been viewed throughout much of Christian history and to the belief that Christians should prevent its occurrence in the wider society. In much Catholic thought, in fact, suicide has been regarded as a mortal sin, an act that can only be condemned and never forgiven. These are tremendously harsh judgments. What are the theological and ethical reasons that lead to such conclusions?

Perhaps the most common is the commandment against murder in the Decalogue. Suicide, in this view, is regarded as self-murder and is prohibited. Yet this interpretation of the Sixth Commandment is not without problems. In Christian tradition, certain instances of killing have often been justified—in "just" wars, or in capital punishment. That which is prohibited is murder, not justifiable killing. Might there be instances in which suicide is not self-murder but justified killing of oneself?

The deeper reasons for negative ethical judgments about suicide are found in a theological affirmation of God as creator and redeemer of human life. Human beings are created in the image of God, so they should not treat others or themselves in any way that violates anyone's personhood. Life is given us as a gift from God. We are to be stewards of this gift. We do not own our lives. Our lives do not belong to us but to God.

Suicide in this understanding is to reject God's gift. It is to take life into one's own hands rather than entrusting it to God. It is to reject God's grace, which is available to persons in the most difficult of circumstances. It is to place oneself in the place of God, making oneself sovereign, rather than accepting the sovereignty of the Creator and Redeemer of all. Often in the past, suicide has been viewed as the ultimate act of rebellion against the authority of God. It is the epitome of human defiance in the face of God's gracious providence.

Two influential Protestant interpreters of suicide in this century are Dietrich Bonhoeffer and Karl Barth. Bonhoeffer regarded suicide as a lack of faith. Instead of trusting in God's grace, the person who commits suicide engages in an act of self-justification. The self is made the center, not God. Barth also generally regarded suicide as unjustifiable, although not as a lack of faith but as the rejection of God's grace, yet he believed there might be exceptions in which God commands suicide; for example, in instances of martyrdom. However, how one really knows when God commands such a thing or how one might distinguish between the voice of God and other voices remains a confusing part of Barth's ethics.

Yet neither Barth nor Bonhoeffer were judgmental toward persons who committed suicide. Barth clearly believed God's mercy extended to acts of suicide. Against much Christian thought, he argued that suicide may be forgiven. Human travails must be recognized. It is wrong to evaluate a person's faith and life by the moment of suicide alone.[5] In these two theologians one encounters the traditional Christian negative judgment about suicide but also a less judgmental and more compassionate recognition of human frailties. Shifts are already occurring.

Utilitarian Ethics

These ways of dealing theologically and ethically with suicide may be contrasted with more utilitarian views that have become increasingly influential in recent years. In theological circles, the work of Joseph Fletcher is especially noteworthy. For Fletcher, love is the only absolute in ethics. This love is grounded in the love of God and is to be expressed in decisions that best serve the well-being of persons.

This approach rejects deterministic views of God and interpretations of God's sovereignty that limit or negate human freedom. Human beings are created with possibilities for self-creation, rationality, and freedom—all to be guided by the norm of love. In Fletcher's writings about biomedical ethics, he has consistently stressed the moral autonomy of the patient. This leads him to affirm the person's capacity and right to choose death in situations of terminal illness and disintegrative suffering—which would include the right to choose suicide.

Fletcher draws the familiar distinction between the quality of life and the quantity of life, arguing that mere survival or self-preservation is not sufficient. Quality of life is a higher value and can provide the basis for defending suicide as a moral option. Love for persons may include supporting the availability of this option and supporting persons who wish to choose it. Fletcher contends it does not have to be only noble reasons that justify suicide "but just because life happens to be too sour or bare," and he concludes, in his characteristically epigrammatic way:

> The full circle is being drawn. In classical times suicide was a tragic option for human dignity's sake. Then for centuries it was a sin. Then it became a crime. Then a sickness. Soon it will become a choice again. Suicide is the signature of freedom.[6]

While Fletcher clearly calls for respecting the reasons why persons may be led to the act of suicide, other utilitarians would provide a more limited justification. They would regard suicide as moral when it is done for the good of others—or, in other words, when it would have beneficial social consequences. In this way of thinking, for example, suicide to relieve family members from the financial or emotional burdens of prolonged illness could be justified. Also, while Fletcher's ethic would lead to more permissive attitudes about suicide in American society, other utilitarians might argue that greater acceptance of suicide could have destructive social consequences. Therefore, intervention to prevent suicides could be justified on utilitarian grounds.[7]

Relational Ethics

We have looked at traditional negative evaluations of suicide and some more recent utilitarian arguments that provide possibilities for justifying suicide, at least in some cases. A third theological and ethical perspective on suicide may be called relational ethics. It relies heavily on the thought of H. Richard Niebuhr. This approach focuses neither on commandments that prescribe or prohibit action nor on goals toward which persons are to direct actions. Instead, it emphasizes the importance of a person's interpretation of what is presented in the situation, and it stresses the priority of personal character over rational deliberation in a person's decision-making. As Niebuhr argued, biblical ethics is not concerned primarily with the question of what rules to obey or which goals to achieve. The central question of biblical ethics is, "What is happening?"[8] In this approach to religious ethics, one's interpretation is shaped by the conviction that one is ultimately accountable to God. One is to make that decision which best fits with the pattern of God's relation with oneself and the world. The moral implication is to relate to others in ways appropriate to God's relation with them and relate to ourselves in ways appropriate to God's relation with us. Standards of love, mercy, and justice are based on and derive their meaning from convictions about God's ways with persons.

And God's ways are dynamic and varied, not frozen or distilled into rules for behavior.

The question may be raised, "Whose interpretation of the situation and action is decisive?" This becomes particularly pertinent in dealing with the ethics of suicide. In some Christian ethical theory, great attention is given to a formal, deductive pattern of moral reasoning, moving from theological beliefs to ethical principles to a moral conclusion. One might, for example, identify belief in God the Creator, which leads to the ethical principle of stewardship of life, which in turn leads to the conclusion that suicide is morally wrong.

The major defect in this approach to ethics is its remoteness from the lived experience of the decision-maker. It is an abstract theory of ethics that may be used to judge "a class of actions" without regard for the factors that weigh heavily on the subject.[9] Instead, interpreters of relational ethics regard pastoral sensitivity to the struggles of persons in the context of a Christian theological perspective as a surer beginning point for moral reflection than formal syllogisms. Whose interpretation is decisive? In relational ethics the answer is the moral subject, the agent of action.

In providing an ethical assessment of suicide, therefore, one needs to consider it primarily from the standpoint of the agent rather than the observer. Persons should be very cautious about rendering a moral judgment from the outside, external to the meanings of the act for the person who chooses it. How is suicide to be interpreted theologically? Perhaps, far from being an arrogant act of rebellion against God, suicide is an agonizing admission of finitude, an incapacity to respond to sources of hope that could overcome despair. In the experience of radical limitation, perhaps one cannot act on other alternatives. The mercy of God in death may seem to be preferable to an impotence to cope with life that the agent experiences in the weakness of his or her finitude. As Lewis Smedes puts it, "Most people who commit suicide see themselves not as storming heaven but as sliding into the abyss."[10] Similarly, suicide in the terminally ill may be anything but a lack of faith in the grace and power of God. In choosing death such persons may be accepting the reality of their finitude and trusting in the grace of God, which encompasses them in death as in life.

The suicides of Elizabeth and Henry Pitney Van Dusen in 1975 raised with particular clarity and force the question of theological interpretation and ethical justification. The two of them together chose suicide. He was seventy-seven years old, and she was eighty. Elizabeth Van Dusen left the following letter:

> To all Friends and Relations,
>
> We hope that you will understand what we have done even though some of you will disapprove of it and some be disillusioned by it.
>
> We have both had very full and satisfying lives.
>
> Pitney has worked hard and with great dedication for the church. I have had an adventurous and happy life. We have both had happy lives, and our children have crowned this happiness.
>
> But since Pitney had his stroke five years ago, we have not been able to do any of the things we want to do and *are* able to do, and my arthritis is much worse.
>
> There are too many helpless old people who without modern medical care would have died, and we feel God would have allowed them to die when their time had come.
>
> Nowadays it is difficult to die. We feel that this way we are taking will become more usual and acceptable as the years pass.
>
> Of course the thought of our children and our grandchildren *make* us sad, but we still feel that this is the best way and the right way to go. We are both increasingly weak and unwell and who would want to die in a Nursing Home.
>
> We are not afraid to die.
>
> We send you all our love and gratitude for your wonderful support and friendship.
>
> "O Lamb of God that takest away the sins of the world Have mercy on us. O Lamb of God that takest away the sins of the world Grant us thy peace."[11]

These words are profoundly moving. They also provide insight into ways suicide may be understood by persons of demonstrated Christian faith and character. Here the Van Dusens express the meaning of their act in the context of their faith and life. It is symbolic of the love and mutual responsibility of the covenant relationship they shared in marriage. They accept accountability not only for the act itself but also for the interpretation of their action. They acknowledge the difficulties their decision will create for others even as they express gratitude for the relationships of family and friends. They affirm the relational context of their decision even as they accept responsibility for it in light of their negative assessment of their future. They act with confidence in the rightness of their decision while expressing humility in their dependence on the mercy and peace of God.

The interpretation of suicide from the standpoint of the subject is not often stated as clearly and profoundly as this. Still, for the agent, as James Gustafson points out, the explanation of the suicide "is the justification, and the justification is the explanation."[12] For those who might bring an observer's perspective to a suicide, the primary moral requirement is not to evaluate the action but to seek empathetically to understand the action from the agent's point of view.

Two influential contemporary interpreters of the relational approach to Christian ethics have written about suicide, Stanley Hauerwas and James Gustafson. Their views bear close attention, as much for the sharp differences between them as for their similarities.

Ethical perspective of Stanley Hauerwas. Hauerwas argues that the Christian interpretation of suicide should be based on the narrative of biblical faith. This narrative does not give rise to moral rules or methods of resolving dilemmas so much as it shapes the character of persons who live within its determinative influence. Hauerwas's insistence on the normative significance of Christian narrative is an attempt to reclaim the centrality of theology for Christian ethics from more utilitarian and psychological interpretations. He clearly believes Christians have too easily accepted contemporary justifications for choosing death as responses to suffering and to severe physical, cognitive, and emotional disabilities. In his view persons who see their lives in relation to the narrative of Christian faith will not regard suicide as a morally justifiable option. Unlike some more traditional moral arguments, this is so not because suicide is a violation of certain prohibitions but because it is incompatible with a Christian interpretation of life.[13] The crux of Hauerwas's argument is:

> In other words, our unwillingness to kill ourselves even under pain is an affirmation that the trust that has sustained us in health is also the trust that sustains us in illness and distress; that our existence is a gift ultimately bounded by a hope that gives us a way to go on; that the full, present memory of our Christian story is a source of strength and consolation for ourselves and our community.[14]

Suicide is incompatible with Christian character for various reasons. It is a denial of the gift character of life, of a trusting relation with God, and of faithfulness toward others with whom we share community. A Christian interpretation, correspondingly, will stress that the meaning of life is to be found in the service of God and in trusting in God's purposes and care in the midst of suffering and dying as in times of health and vitality. A Christian interpretation will stress the communal character of personal existence and the need for mutual trust, forgiveness, and commitment in relationships. As suicide may represent the "metaphysical I-gotcha"[15] of a person's anger and bitterness, it may also represent the failure of the community to the person. Suicide should not be justified morally because it is contrary to what Christians affirm about life. Whatever the reasons might be that motivate persons to kill themselves, doing so communicates meanings that are incompatible with the narrative that shapes the Christian life.

Hauerwas recognizes that current medical treatments may prolong dying beyond the time required by a Christian affirmation of life. At a certain point the acceptance of death and the refusal of further treatment may be an expression of trust in God's care. Still, Hauerwas is less concerned with such instances than in conveying the conviction that courage to live faithfully in the face of suffering is integral to Christian character.

Since the question of suicide is frequently raised in the context of disintegrative suffering and terminal illness, these circumstances are more central to an ethical assessment of suicide than Hauerwas acknowledges. There are no particular reasons why accepting the reality of death in reliance on the grace and mercy of God and acting on that acceptance is incompatible with affirming the gift character of life and one's responsibility to and for others. Choosing death rather than prolonged dying may express confidence in the faithfulness of God and rejection of the death denial of modern medicine and culture. The Christian narrative provides varied ways to interpret decisions for suicide that may qualify more than Hauerwas grants by his generally negative assessment.

Hauerwas further makes it clear that his interpretation and assessment of suicide is not intended to be judgmental toward persons who kill themselves. He is not interested in exploring the reasons why persons are unable or unwilling to accept the narrative of biblical faith and, instead, choose suicide. More important, to him, is to convey the normative character of Christian ethics in such a way that persons so orient themselves toward life and death that suicide is not considered a moral alternative. Hauerwas's interpretation is an important response to those who regard meaningful life to be dependent on boundless health, keen intelligence, and occupational productivity. Yet the relation of the normative story of life-affirming existence to those persons who are deeply afflicted needs to be brought into Hauerwas's interpretive framework. Decisions for suicide arising from despair require more interpretation than the sweeping moral assessment that they are incompatible with Christian ethics.

Ethical perspective of James Gustafson. Unlike Hauerwas, James Gustafson gives primary attention to the dynamics of despair in his interpretation of the ethics of suicide. He does not contend that this provides the only way to understand suicide, but he does believe despair is frequently at the heart of the matter. Often despair best accounts for the most sad and tragic instances in which persons kill themselves. We may be able to justify the suicide of persons who choose death instead of a prolonged period of physical and mental deterioration or terminal illness, as hard as it may be. But it is more difficult to deal with the suicides of adolescents and adults with seemingly much for which to live.

Despair points to a spiritual condition. Persons may be so

afflicted with hopelessness that they cannot envision anything positive about the future. They can only see the worst. Despair cannot be overcome merely by rational arguments from others, pointing out various hopeful alternatives, or by appeals to the will such as "Pull yourself out of it" or "Why don't you try this [or do that]?" Despair makes it difficult if not impossible to experience subjectively the meaningfulness of life that is central to Christian faith and ethics.

Gustafson describes despair in eight ways, seeking to develop a moral phenomenology of the afflictions of persons that may lead them to choose suicide. In brief, despair can come from a sense of impossibility or fatedness, or from a deep conflict of loyalties. Despair may spring from aimlessness or from the loss of one's sense of self-determination. Isolation can bring about despair, as can an excessive sense of moral scrupulosity. Despair may be evoked by "deadly seriousness" or by a seeming lack of sources of forgiveness.[16]

What implications does this analysis of despair have for ethical reflections about suicide? To begin with, there is an intriguing and important shift in the way we might deal with the ethics of suicide. Gustafson changes the moral focus from the person who commits suicide to the relational environment on which all persons depend. His analysis of the dynamics of despair leads to an attitude of empathy toward the person who chooses suicide, by recognizing the conditions that lead the person to believe this is the only thing to do. To other persons, his analysis provides insights into their moral responsibility for nurturing relationships in which the despair that prompts suicide is less likely.

This shift in orientation is rooted in his theological perspective. Gustafson asks the question, What is God enabling and requiring us to do? The appropriate response is that persons are to participate in patterns of relationship in ways that lessen the likelihood of despair and nourish sources of hope and renewal. More specifically, moral responsibility to others in the complex web of relationship means to nurture and support sources of *hope,* which lessen persons' sense of fatedness; of *healing,* which reduces the conflict of divided loyalties; of *purpose,* which overcomes aimlessness; of *self-determination,* which replaces the sense of futility; of *relationships,* which overcome isolation; of *acceptance of finitude,* which relieves persons from misplaced guilt; of *joy,* which lessens deadly seriousness; and of *forgiveness,* which lifts the burdens of moral wrongs. In these ways persons minister to one another, nourishing those gifts in relationship that are sources for life and for preventing or relieving despair.

Concluding Reflections

Many people have noted the high incidence of suicide in the United States and asked what this may reveal about the quality of relationships in this society. If Gustafson is right, Americans are not doing very well in sustaining the kinds of relationships in which persons can experience meaning, forgiveness, joy, and hope. The key moral task, then, is not the evaluation of the act of suicide but the cultivation of qualities that deepen and enrich personal relationships.

Not only may suicides reveal serious weaknesses and wrongs in primary relationships, they also point to social sources of hopelessness. The number of suicides among American Indians is extraordinarily high, reflecting the despair bred by the conditions of oppression under which they live. Recent incidences of suicides by farmers reflect the despair bred by loss of farms and deep indebtedness. The increase in suicides among teenagers that some have called epidemic may reflect the despair bred by the lack of opportunities for broader social participation in which they might experience the meaning, empowerment, and hope of historical action. The moral implication of this interpretation is to overcome the social sources of hopelessness and impotence that breed despair through fundamental social change: that is, to make the social environment genuinely life-affirming.

In the relational ethical approach to suicide, the moral autonomy of the individual is not the most relevant characteristic of the person. To be sure, respect for persons' capacities to make decisions is important. But we are always persons in relation. Persons are morally obligated to take others into account in their decision-making. They are obligated to attend to the patterns and environments of relationship in which persons are required to make decisions. I am to make my own decisions, yes—but always in interaction with those to whom I am most closely related, with those who are most directly affected, and with that wider community of persons with whom I share responsibility for shaping a common ethos. In bonds of love and care, we have responsibilities beyond merely supporting one another's individual choices.

It is within this relational matrix that we need to deal with the ethics of suicide. In a Christian perspective, we are to do what God is enabling and requiring us to do—to nourish in one another and in our communities the spiritual and moral qualities that sustain persons in life and prevent the affliction of despair. In this sense, the chief element of moral responsibility is suicide prevention. While this certainly requires many different kinds of efforts, at its most basic level it requires attention to the quality of relationships and life opportunities that get at the roots of despair.

Does this relational approach to suicide, then, lead to the conclusion that friends and family bear the most responsibility for the suicide of a loved one? Or does the person who commits suicide bear the responsibility for the afflictions that lead him or her to such an action? Or must society itself be held responsible? This is a difficult and complex question. One cannot say that others, including wider communities, are the direct cause of the despair that leads to suicide. But one cannot necessarily say that the individual is fully responsible either.

In relational ethics, persons are responsible to and for one another, especially those with whom they are in special covenants of intimacy. They share responsibility for the quality of relationship. There is a degree of mutually shared responsibility for one another's spiritual and moral condition. Yet this is by no means to say that family and friends are fully or directly accountable for the loved one's despair. Many persons have experienced at some time the agony of impotence in seeking to bring sources of healing and hope to loved ones. We are limited by our own finiteness as well as by our moral failures. We are also limited by the "otherness" of the one who has dimensions of personhood beyond our reach.

Yet we do need to stress our moral responsibility to nurture relationships and establish social conditions in which afflictions are less likely or may be overcome. Family and friends of a person who has chosen suicide need pastoral resources that enable them not only to grieve over their loss but also to accept their finitude and receive forgiveness for their wrongs. Much guilt may be exaggerated and itself a source for despair. But guilt does not emerge only from the notion of a punitive God or from a perfectionist conscience. Rather, it may also emerge from the recognition that we are inextricably bound together and bear responsibility for one another. Not denial but forgiveness is the appropriate response to our moral failures with one another and with God.

What about the responsibility of the person who chooses suicide? Gustafson argues in a convincing way that this person often is not fully accountable for the afflictions that lead to suicide.[17] Factors and forces may close in that are beyond the capacities of the person to cope with. There may even be powerful reasons for the despair. Despair sometimes has a way of becoming overwhelming. "The tragedy of their deaths," in Gustafson's words, "flows from conditions of life beyond their powers to control."[18]

Yet Gustafson may not emphasize sufficiently the responsibility of persons to develop patterns of relationship that prevent despair in themselves as well as in others. While this is implied in his discussion, it needs to be developed further. That is, one is more likely to be susceptible to despair if one isolates oneself from others, if one becomes so obligation-oriented one cannot enjoy life, and if one cuts oneself off from contexts in which one can experience forgiveness and the power of renewal.

One has the moral responsibility to cultivate in oneself those capacities to receive the gift of life and participate in it gratefully. One has the moral responsibility to invest oneself in contexts and relationships that sustain hope and overcome tendencies to despair. In Christian understandings the church is to be a community of meaning, empowerment, forgiveness, and hope. It is important to invest oneself in its life—for the sake of God, others, and oneself—to explore and experience what God is enabling persons to become together.

What conclusions, then, may be drawn from this ethical inquiry into suicide?

First is the obligation to prevent suicides, both by direct intervention and by nurturing relationships that sustain persons in life.[19] Suicide is obviously an irreversible act. It ends life. There is no second chance to change one's mind or open oneself to resources that might make life bearable. Presumptions for protecting and sustaining life provide a warrant for preventing persons from committing suicide if we are able. This is not to say, however, that there are not instances when a person's choice for suicide should be supported rather than prevented. Persons like the Van Dusens, with afflictions related to advanced age, or persons with terminal illnesses come most readily to mind.

Second, the obligation to prevent suicides also requires removing the social sources of hopelessness that breed despair in many persons. Stated more positively, the moral requirement is to nourish the social ethos and to establish the societal structures in which persons may experience the meaning and potentialities of life. The empowerment of persons to be involved in shaping the conditions of their lives and the character of the wider society is particularly pivotal in engendering hope. Suicide prevention involves responsibilities for social change as well as interpersonal relations.

Third, after the moral responsibility to prevent suicides and the conditions from which they spring, is the moral responsibility to empathize with the person who chose suicide and to understand the reasons from that agent's point of view. Here Gustafson's discussion is particularly helpful. He argues that though suicide is always a tragic moral choice, it may also be a justifiable one in light of the person's afflictions. For friends and families, the implication is to consent to the suicide. If there is no other choice that a person is able to make in the face of unbearable and unrelievable suffering, we should "consent to its being done."[20]

Fourth, the ethical responsibility remains to provide ministries of pastoral care with persons who have experienced the loss of a loved one through suicide. While the discipline of pastoral care may provide the most significant insights about how

to express compassion and support, it is important to emphasize that this ministry of care is a crucial dimension of a Christian perspective on the ethics of suicide—to provide that
relational context in which such persons can deal with their
own affliction and receive sources of strength for their own
living.

NOTES

1. See James Gustafson, *Ethics from a Theocentric Perspective,* vol. 2 (Chicago: University of Chicago Press, 1984), p.
201; also Jerry Jacobs, *The Moral Justification of Suicide*
(Springfield, Ill.: Charles C Thomas, 1982), p. 136.

2. For discussions of the definition of suicide, see Donald S.
Klinefelter, "The Morality of Suicide," *Soundings* 67(3):337–
338 (Fall 1984); Glenn C. Graber, "The Rationality of Suicide," in *Suicide and Euthanasia,* ed. S. E. Wallace and A. Eser
(Knoxville, Tenn.: University of Tennessee Press, 1981), pp.
51–58; and James Childress, *Who Should Decide?* (New York:
Oxford University Press, 1982), p. 180. Childress argues it is
not only the intention of a person that defines suicide but also
"who performs the *final* act that brings about death." This, for
Childress, is what differentiates assisted suicide from active
voluntary euthanasia.

3. Graber, "Rationality of Suicide," pp. 57–58.

4. Quoted by James T. Clemons in "Suicide and Christian
Moral Judgment," *Christian Century,* May 8, 1985, p. 467,
from *The Works of John Wesley* (Grand Rapids: Baker Book
House, 1979), vol. 13, p. 481.

5. See Gustafson's discussion of Bonhoeffer's and Barth's
views of suicide in *Ethics,* vol. 2, pp. 187–192.

6. Joseph Fletcher, "In Defense of Suicide," in *Suicide and
Euthanasia,* p. 50.

7. See Gustafson's discussion of John Stuart Mill and
Henry Sidgwick in *Ethics,* pp. 194–195.

8. H. Richard Niebuhr, *The Responsible Self* (New York:
Harper & Row, 1963), p. 67.

9. See Gustafson's critique of Thomas Aquinas's treatment of suicide on this particular point in *Ethics,* p. 193.

10. Lewis B. Smedes, "Morality and Suicide," *Reformed Journal,* Jan. 1983, p. 11.

11. Quoted from Klinefelter, "Morality of Suicide," pp. 345–346.

12. Gustafson, *Ethics,* p. 199.

13. The outline and implications of Stanley Hauerwas's interpretation of Christian ethics may be seen in his writings on diverse themes and topics. His perspective on the ethics of suicide is provided in an essay written with Richard Bondi and David B. Burrell, "Memory, Community, and the Reasons for Living: Reflections on Suicide and Euthanasia," in *Truthfulness and Tragedy* (Notre Dame, Ind.: University of Notre Dame Press, 1977), pp. 101–115.

14. Ibid., p. 111.

15. Ibid., pp. 112–113. This is the authors' colorful way to describe suicide as "the ultimate revenge."

16. See Gustafson for these interpretations of the dynamics of despair that often accompany the choice of suicide, *Ethics,* pp. 198–207.

17. Ibid., p. 201.

18. Ibid., p. 209.

19. See Gustafson, *Ethics,* p. 215; also Childress, *Who Should Decide?,* p. 162.

20. Gustafson, *Ethics,* pp. 215–216.

5

Ethical Perspectives for the Community

J. Philip Wogaman

J. PHILIP WOGAMAN, an ordained United Methodist minister, is Professor of Christian Ethics at Wesley Theological Seminary, Washington, D.C., a post he has occupied since 1966. From 1972 to 1983 he also served as dean of that institution. His ten published books include *Christian Perspectives on Politics, Christian Moral Judgment,* and *Faith and Fragmentation: Christianity for a New Age.*

A past president of the Society of Christian Ethics of the United States and Canada, Wogaman is also a member of the American Theological Society, the World Methodist Council, and the Board of Directors of the Churches' Center for Theology and Public Policy. He was a delegate to the 1988 General Conference of The United Methodist Church.

George Santayana has written that "existence is a miracle and, morally considered, a free gift from moment to moment."[1] This observation is an intriguing note on which to begin an ethical discussion of the problem of suicide for two reasons.

First, it raises a question that is not often considered: Is it even *possible* to commit suicide? There is no doubt that people can destroy their physical bodies. But whether we can destroy our selfhood is another question. We did not choose to be in the first place, and it may be an open question whether we can ultimately choose not to be. Our existence is something that has happened to us by a power beyond us. We do not *know* that we can cause our own nonexistence. H. Richard Niebuhr asks the question this way:

> Though I wish to be mortal, if the power that threw me into being in this mortal destructible body elects me into being again there is nothing I can do about that. I can destroy the life of my body. Can I destroy myself? This remains the haunting question of the literature of suicide and of all the lonely debates of men [and women] to whom existence is a burden. Whether they shall wake up again, either here in this life or there in some other mode of being, is beyond their control. We can choose among many alternatives; but the power to choose self-existence or self-extinction is not ours.[2]

Putting the matter even more bluntly, it is not certain that the act of suicide will improve one's situation. Still, most people are inclined to base their thinking on clearly observable consequences. And death, as a consequence of suicide, is clearly observable! But what happens to the *essential self* remains a mystery.

The second point made by the Santayana quotation is that our lives are not simply our own property. Our existence is a gift from whatever power it is that governs reality. We are ultimately responsible to that source of our being. That is the level at which the issue of suicide is joined theologically. And without establishing that point, suicide cannot be approached as an issue in Christian ethics. Let us examine this idea first before proceeding to an ethical analysis of suicide as such.

The Gift of Life

Santayana's point, which he pursued philosophically, is one of the real fundamentals of Christian theology. Human life is the gift of the creator, but the gift is more than the possibility of pursuing an individual human existence. The gift is existence plus relationship. God, having given us the gift of life, affirms our being and invites us into loving relationship. Through the person and work of Christ we are given to understand that God loves each of us without qualification. Nothing we have done or can do destroys God's love for us; it is that radical. The estrangement of human beings from God is from the human side, not from God's side.

The point, echoing Santayana, is that we belong to God, not just to ourselves. Yet in this belonging we are as beloved children, not simply things, or even servants (as the parable of the prodigal son of Luke 15:11–32 is intended to convey). Paul's characteristic admonition to Christians is that they are "called to belong to Jesus Christ" (Rom. 1:6; see also Gal. 5:24). To belong to Jesus Christ is to have one's life grounded in grace: that is, in the wholehearted, unmerited love of God as experienced through Christ.

There is also a human dimension of belonging. We have our being in community, not simply as individuals. Our belonging to God establishes at the deepest level our belonging also to one another. The divine-human covenant thus also creates the community of the covenant. The gift of our lives, therefore, is not just to ourselves but also to the community of humankind of which we are a part. The imagery of John Donne's phrase "No man is an island" suggests that we are all literally a part of one another's lives—and when one is lost, all are diminished. While that point can be registered on an altogether humanistic level, it receives its most powerful expression in the faith that we are all a part of one another's lives because we all belong first to the life of God. This is the foundation point from which Christian discussion of the morality of suicide begins.

What Is Suicide?

Such a foundation point does not, on the face of it, exclude the possibility of suicide, but it does require us to see it as a more than personal act. To conclude that one's own life has become intolerably painful is to address the possibility of suicide on an individualistic level. Later, I will address the corporate and pastoral implications of relating to persons confronting what the mystics called the "dark night of the soul." And it should be clear that when one brings the intolerability of pain, spiritual or physical, directly into the relationship one has with God and one's fellows—either a psalmist's lament, a "primal scream," or a simple petition for human help—this is not "individualistic" or even necessarily self-centered. It is pain considered in relationship. But to conclude, within oneself, that the pain has become too great and to contemplate the taking of one's own life as a result—that is to raise the question of whether one is thinking and acting within the covenant with God and with one's sisters and brothers of the human community.

The import of this is most evident in the pain that a successful suicide so often inflicts on loved ones. Moreover, the effects of suicide can ripple broadly across the community, creating higher "suicide-expectancy."[3] The act, while prompted by deep personal pain, also inflicts pain. It can scarcely remain an altogether individual deed.

Nor can it be, in Christian terms, a deed of "honor." It cannot be a way of making amends for one's moral failures, in the manner of the samurai who, having failed in battle or other social responsibility, could only reestablish their lost personal dignity and integrity by falling on their swords. It is not, in Christian terms, a way of social restoration. For one thing, Christians understand that *all* "have sinned and fall short of the glory of God" (Rom. 3:23). Paul, who records this, also notes the deeply Christian response to our human moral failures: that we "are justified by his grace as a gift" (v. 24). To be Christian is to understand not only that we stand in need of forgiveness but that we are also capable of receiving it. Viewed from this perspective, Bonhoeffer may be right in suggesting that "suicide is the ultimate and extreme self-justification of man as man."[4] It is taking into one's own hands the question of the ultimate meaning of one's life, not trusting it to God. At the least, suicide undertaken to reestablish one's honor is conceding an ultimacy to the community that it does not properly have apart from God.

What, then, is suicide? Karl Barth bluntly characterizes it as a form of murder:

> To deprive a man of his life is a matter for the One who gave it and not for the man himself. He who takes what does not belong to him, in this case only to throw it away, does not merely kill; he murders. There is no ground on which to justify or authorise this.

For it is not even for man himself to decide whether his existence
is a success or a failure, whether it is tolerable or intolerable,
whether its continuation is possible or impossible, far less
whether it is worth while or mean and worthless. The Creator,
Giver, and Lord of life decides all these things, and no one else.[5]

Suicide as a Personal Moral Decision

Barth's judgment of suicide, as a personal moral decision, is
categorically negative. This simply is not something a faithful
Christian can do. Is he right about this? Are there any circumstances that justify a Christian in taking his or her own life?

Notice that this way of putting the question subtly changes
the frame of reference. Where we have previously been speaking of suicide in the context of God's gift of existence and
grace, now we are using more legalistic language as we speak of
whether or not this is a deed that can be justified. I emphasize
this point because above all else, for Christians, suicide must
continue to be seen in the light of faith and the loving, gracious
relationship with God. So let us rephrase the question. Are
there any circumstances under which suicide best fulfills God's
loving intentions for us? And, therefore, are there circumstances under which it is well for Christians to consider taking
their own lives?

Two kinds of situation can be excluded as not being deliberate deeds in the sense these questions imply. First, the
self-sacrificial act of one who dies for others or for a cause em-
bodying the love of God is not really "suicide." In an earlier
writing,[6] I recounted the story of an acquaintance who entered
a burning house to save his wife and mother-in-law, not knowing that they, meanwhile, had escaped through the back door.
The man later died as a result of burns suffered through this
deed of needless heroism. The act was possibly reckless, even
foolhardy, but it was not done because the man wished to destroy himself. In wartime, soldiers have been known to throw
themselves on live grenades in order to save the lives of their
comrades. Presumably, they are overjoyed in those instances
when the grenades do not explode. Jesus himself apparently
could have avoided the circumstances leading to his crucifix-

ion, but we would scarcely classify his death on the cross as suicide. Self-sacrificial deeds can be done in the full knowledge that inevitably they will cause one's own death. But that does not make them suicide.

One must also acknowledge the desperate irrationality of many suicides. And one surely does not stand in judgment of those who have acted out of uncontrollable despair. Most of the suicides I have known personally have been of this sort. And in most of these cases it is difficult even to imagine a cool, rational conversation before the act in which we might have reflected together on the Christian faithfulness of the deed— even if there had been opportunity for such a conversation.

But are there situations in which such a conversation is conceivable, and in which the conclusion ought to be that, yes, one should take one's own life?

I am reluctant to state an absolute negative to that, but it seems clear, in light of the faith of Christians, that the burden of proof should weigh heavily against it. That is to say, in any particular instance there should be very weighty reasons before one should conclude that one should take one's own life. What kinds of reasons should count?

Suicide and Human Suffering

Should unendurable physical or psychological pain count as an adequate reason for suicide? That is the reason most often stated by those who urge greater acceptance of suicide as an option. The ancient Epicureans, for whom the moral life consisted of the maximization of pleasure and the minimization of pain, were consistent in affirming the option of suicide. One of them, the poet Lucretius, wrote:

> If, one day, as well may happen, life grows wearisome, there only remains to pour a libation to death and oblivion. A drop of subtle poison will gently close your eyes to the sun and waft you smiling into the eternal night whence everything comes and to which everything returns.[7]

Echoing this theme in her own way, Mary Rose Barrington, a British lawyer, speaks of suicide or euthanasia as a rational response to "an apparently irremediable state of physical debility that makes life unbearable to the sufferer."[8] And, in justifying suicide when based on "a realistic assessment" of one's "life situation," psychiatrist Jerome A. Motto clearly understands by this that the situation is one of intolerable pain—a "truly unendurable existence."[9] Is unendurable pain a good reason for ending one's own life?

One problem is that even a brief period of pain can be unendurable. All of us have experienced moments of intense, searing physical pain—a migraine headache, catching one's finger in the car door, a severe burn, a blow to the shin, childbirth—when absolutely *anything* to bring it to an end would be welcome. And all of us have experienced moments of deep emotional depression, of a spiritual pain worse, if anything, than its physical counterpart. Such pain may be temporary. But a decision for suicide in the midst of the pain will be permanent in its effects.

Still, pain can be unremitting, and there are some forms of terminal illness from which death is the only known respite apart from increasingly inadequate medications. When somebody faced with this chooses suicide, I don't believe others should stand in judgment.

But contrary to the Epicurean philosophy, neither pleasure nor pain defines quality of life as perceived by Christians. The *meaning* of life transcends both the physical and emotional content of our feelings. To be sure, nobody seeks pain, and everybody takes pleasure in pleasure. It is good to feel good; it is bad to feel bad. But there is something deeper than that, for the sake of which one can even choose to endure pain. Paul wrote that he was sure "that neither death, nor life, nor angels, nor principalities, nor things present, nor things to come, nor power, nor height, nor depth, nor anything else in all creation, will be able to separate us from the love of God in Christ Jesus our Lord" (Rom. 8:38–39). That statement, of course, relativizes death; and on the basis of that one could say the taking of one's own life is not to separate oneself from the love of God. This, I believe, is to be affirmed. But at the same time, the realization of that inalienable love of God is an invitation to respond courageously to every circumstance of life.

Courage to live in the face of what others call unendurable pain is itself a powerful witness to the love of God and thereby a great gift of love to those who see. A decision for suicide, on the other hand, communicates the ultimacy of pain. Those who have had pastoral experience with people of great courage at the frontiers of suffering know what a powerful witness this can be.[10] We have also known people who simply could not endure, and they too are upheld in the love of God. This is not to "justify" suicide but to say that, in the face of unimaginable pain, it is not to be condemned.

Suicide and Human Dignity

The literature on suicide is also loaded with suggestions that suicide can be the way to preserve one's own honor and dignity as a human being. The ancient Stoic writer Seneca, in a celebrated essay on suicide, remarked that "mere living is not a good, but living well . . . and dying well means escape from the danger of living ill."[11] In this essay Seneca is critical of a prisoner of the tyrant Lysimachus of Rhodes who refused the option of suicide on the grounds that "A man may hope for anything while he has life." Seneca regarded this as "a shameful confession of weakness."[12] Some have regarded it as similarly shameful to continue to live after having disgraced themselves in some way. And discussions of suicide, as of euthanasia, include references to the human desire to avoid a lingering death in which one's dignity is lost. The idea that one might be reduced to total dependency, perhaps with severe loss of mental and physical capacities, seems alien to our basic humanness and self-respect.

On one level this does need to be taken seriously. In many cultures, suicide is considered an honorable way out for those who have disgraced themselves.[13] Within the context of such cultures, suicide is arguably an ultimate way of preserving one's dignity. Similarly, some cultures (such as our own?) do place a high premium on independence, rationality, and aesthetic appearances, and suicide is a way of preserving one's independence in the face of the likelihood of physical and mental deterioration.

But this is to view life in a very individualistic way. Christian faith sees life in communal, covenantal, interdependent ways. We all belong together, in a great human family, because we belong to God. Within that family, dignity is known to derive from our relationship to God, not primarily from the face we can put on our relations with others. Moreover, within that family of God there is no ultimate disgrace. Indeed, the Christian perspective well understands that all of us are sinners, and no one can be presumed more so or less so than the others. That is for God, the gracious giver of all good, to decide. Nor can the loss of mental or bodily functions be taken as loss of dignity. In the words of Job, "Naked I came from my mother's womb, and naked shall I return; the LORD gave, and the LORD has taken away; blessed be the name of the LORD" (Job 1:21). Real human dignity has different roots from our physical and mental functions. There is, in fact, a kind of dignity in acceptance of the "gentle curve" that carries us from dependent childhood, through mature active adult years, and back into a more dependent relationship to the community insofar as that proves necessary. In all states of our existence we are part of a social whole that is greater than we are. We make our contributions to the life of the community, but we all receive from it.

Seen in this perspective, I am reluctant to endorse the view of Karen Lebacqz and H. Tristram Engelhardt, Jr., that a suicide pact can be an acceptable expression of covenantal life.[14] For one thing, the two (or more) participants are unlikely to be at the same stage of mental or physical deterioration or pain. For another, the premise of such a pact always seems to be that those who participate belong only to one another, while there is a deeper theological sense in which they belong to all others and to God.

Accordingly, it is difficult to identify or accept the logic of those arguing that suicide can be an assertion or protection of one's human dignity—at least in the ultimate theological context where human dignity can finally be said to matter. However, suicide should not be assumed to have the opposite effect—that is, loss of human dignity. For many people who do not have a deep faith in God's affirming love, the small human tokens of dignity are the only basis they have for self-esteem.

For such a person, living in shame or loss of dignity could contribute to a loss of self-esteem that might be worse than death. But that is to characterize a human tragedy, not the norm of life seen through a grace that transcends the human.

Suicide as an Expression of Love

Each of these reasons for suicide can be taken as an expression of individualism, perhaps even of self-centeredness (though sometimes a thoroughly understandable self-centeredness). One cannot so classify suicide when it is an expression of love. I am not now thinking of the acts of heroism mentioned earlier, for these are not suicidal by intent. The subject here is the suicide of one who has concluded that this is the only way to save his or her family from utter financial ruin in a debilitating illness. Often that may be misguided thinking, since a family may far prefer to have their loved one with them as long as possible. And the suicide may leave the family with a sense of guilt or confusion about why their loved one has taken this extreme measure. Moreover, there is the effect this will have on the wider society. Will it lead others to follow suit? Will it contribute to the notion that the comparative affluence of survivors is more important than the continued life of terminally ill patients? But then again, the objective circumstances may be such that financial ruin would do much more harm than the premature loss of a loved one through suicide.[15] In a truly extreme case, where the disease is clearly terminal and the economic circumstances truly overpowering, the taking of one's own life might be an act of love—but let the burden of proof weigh very heavily against it.

Suicidal acts have also been undertaken to call the community's attention to some vital cause or grave injustice. A young Czech student immolated himself in Czechoslovakia's famed Wenceslaus Square in 1968 to protest the grave injustice of the Soviet invasion of that country. That act did help rally the people of Czechoslovakia and may temporarily have deflected the momentum behind the Soviet occupation. An American similarly immolated himself before the Pentagon to protest the Vietnam War in an act that probably did contribute to the seriousness and resolve, and ultimately the success, of the antiwar movement of the late 1960s and early 1970s. (Several Buddhists monks had anticipated this deed by doing the same thing in the streets of Saigon.) Such acts, particularly if they are not routine, certainly do attract attention. But one wonders whether there aren't similarly dramatic gestures that would not, at the same time, involve bloodshed.

There are other action possibilities that may place one's life in jeopardy but still place the onus of actual loss of life on those one seeks to change. When demonstrators have lain down in front of trucks or locomotives to prevent their movement (with military supplies, for example), this can be a vivid way to call attention to a cause. It can be suicidal in effect, if the trucks or trains run anyway; but that decision is left in the hands of those identified with the policies one is attempting to change. The fasts undertaken by Mohandas K. Gandhi in India—or, more recently, by Mitch Snyder in the United States—are also life-threatening; but such fasts do give those whom one is seeking to change an opportunity to do so without loss of life. So while this kind of act is not necessarily suicidal in effect, it is potentially so. Again, the burden of proof should be against it. One should not do this kind of thing lightly or routinely. One should not do it for motives other than love.

Such illustrations suggest that suicidal actions can, in extreme situations, be undertaken as an act of love, but that they should always be a last resort.

The Responsibility of Christians Toward Potential Suicides

Thus far we have treated the subject as a decision being considered by the one who is contemplating suicide—bearing in mind that such decisions often are not taken in the full possession of one's rational faculties. Now we must ask about the moral responsibilities of those who are in a position to affect a suicidal decision by somebody else.

Surely everybody would agree that a demonstration of empathy and love is the most important thing anybody can do. Nor is that likely to be a mere gesture. I am persuaded that a good deal of clinical depression has a physiological basis, as evidenced by the success of some drugs in dealing with it. Nevertheless, it also seems clear that much psychological depression grows out of a sense of isolation or alienation. People who do not feel that they are loved by others may have very little to live for. Genuine caring can make a difference in many cases. For Christians this is not simply a moral obligation to prevent suicides, it is a whole orientation toward life. In other words, the best way for Christians to help prevent suicides may often be serving as the channels of grace that we are called in faith to be.

Does this mean, then, that when suicides occur it is because Christians have failed? All of us have had to face this haunting question when those we have known as friends or loved ones have taken their own lives or tried to do so. How impossible it can be to sort out the tangled webs of relationship that lie in the wake of successful suicides or suicide attempts! It is a reminder that we *do* fail one another in the life of community; all of us do. And yet we cannot actually *be* that other who has a claim upon our love. In the final analysis, we must accept the reality of a failure in which the whole community is implicated, knowing that all of us depend finally on the inexhaustible grace of God.

What about active intervention to prevent suicide? Some argue that this shows disrespect for the freedom and personhood of the one who contemplates taking his or her own life. Thomas Szasz quotes a Stefan Zweig character's assertion that "among the 'rights of man' there is a right which no one can take away, the right to croak when and where and how one pleases, without a 'helping hand.' "[16] According to Szasz himself, to treat the wish to die as necessarily irrational or pathological, one in fact contributes to "a far-reaching infantilization and dehumanization of the suicidal person." And with some sarcasm he writes that "do-gooders have always opposed personal autonomy or self-determination."[17] Jerome A. Motto suggests that "we must eventually establish procedures for the voluntary cessation of life, with the time, place, and manner largely controlled by the person concerned. . . . It will," he continues, "necessarily involve a series of deliberate steps providing assurance that appropriate criteria are met, such as those proposed above, as we now observe specific criteria when a life is terminated by abortion or by capital punishment." Such procedures would, he anticipates, lead to "a decrease in the actual number of suicides" since "if I know something is available to me and will remain available till I am moved to seize it, the chances of my seizing it now are thereby much reduced. It is only by holding off that I maintain the option of changing my mind."[18]

I am not persuaded by this argument. Given the fact that those who wholeheartedly intend to commit suicide will almost always find a way to succeed, it seems to me that when there is opportunity to intervene one should do so. The intervention will not be permanently successful if the intention is deeply fixed. But on the other hand, a successful suicide will be permanent if not prevented. It may be that intervention only buys time. But time can be the most important thing. Have we not all known people whose suicidal attempts were prevented by others and who now thank God for that timely intervention? On one level this may indeed show disrespect for the personal autonomy of the one in whose life we thus intervene. But it may be the kind of "disrespect" for a person's present state of mind that shows greater regard for the deeper reality of that person's life. The psychological implications of different forms of intervention are beyond the compass of this discussion— and probably beyond its competence as well. But intervention cannot generally be considered ethically objectionable. Quite the contrary: confronted by a potential suicide, our presumption should always be that we ought to intervene unless there are exceptional reasons for not doing so in the particular situation.

The Responsibility of the State

We must also consider the responsibilities of the state. Thinking of the state as society acting as a whole, it really represents all of us; it is the whole community acting together through law and designated officials and agencies. Our discussion thus far has some obvious implications for the state.

First, bearing in mind how the apparent meaninglessness of much life relates to unemployment[19]—with the implication, for the unemployed, that their lives are useless—the state has a very great responsibility to ensure full employment and other opportunities for people to make meaningful contributions to the life of the community.

Second, there is no room for punitive legislation directed at those attempting suicide or at their families or heirs. The history of such legislation and its effects is not a very pretty one, [20] no matter how well intentioned it may have been. Such situations cry out for compassion, not condemnation. Obviously, life insurance companies have a right to put reasonable waivers in their policies to prevent deliberate attempts to gain wealth for one's heirs. And any other direct incentive to suicide should be removed. But this is different from the kind of punitive moralism that has so often infected legislation on the subject in the past.

Third, wherever possible the state should undergird family life with health and welfare legislation, removing potential financial ruin as a rational basis for suicide. That does not mean that vast sums of money should necessarily be expended to keep people alive for briefly extended periods of time. In many cases, a wise and compassionate community will decide that it is time to conclude heroic medical efforts. But after such efforts have ended, and during the remaining period of the patient's life, provision should be made for care so that the burden falls on the community and not only on the patient's loved ones.

Fourth, confronted by an actual suicide attempt, it is normally the state's duty to intervene—physically, if necessary—to buy time. Legislation should, and I believe usually does, make it possible to hold such a person for protective custody and psychological examination without charging the person with a criminal offense.

Fifth, the community as a whole, acting through the state, should ensure that adequate mental health resources are available to help those who can be helped emotionally. That is not to take responsibility away from families, churches, and others acting privately. But neither should we expect governmental agencies to be necessarily impersonal and uncaring. When the people who staff governmental programs are sensitive and compassionate, they well symbolize the best attitudes in the community as a whole. They can be a reminder that the whole community stands together in face of the ultimate issues of life and death and that those who feel alienated and alone really do belong.

The Responsibility of the Church

Finally, the responsibility of the church should be clear. Of all institutions in society, the church is best situated to convey the meaning of life to people who have concluded that, for them, it has lost its meaning. Its gospel is the foundation upon which Durkheim's *anomie* can be challenged. In a complex age such as ours, the church has a great responsibility to be in conversation with different aspects of our culture, helping people to see the patterns of their existence in relation to a deeper faith. And so the church is called to proclaim the gospel of grace and, in its own life, to embody that gospel. It embodies that gospel best when it is particularly solicitous of those within its number who are most troubled and when it reaches beyond its own membership to such people who stand alone.

Few people would now advocate a judgmental attitude on the part of the church—such as sometimes characterized its approach to suicide in the past. Nor can we sustain a judgmental attitude toward the church itself for its failures in reaching out to those who need help. God knows, that has often been our failure, our neglect of the treasures of love of which we are stewards. But we can seize the opportunity we have to be good stewards—and the reality that it is in speaking and being the word of love that we experience in our own lives the depth of what God has given.

NOTES

1. George Santayana, "Ultimate Religion," *Obiter Scripta,* ed. J. Buchler and B. Schwartz (New York: Charles Scribner's Sons, 1936), p. 283.

2. H. Richard Niebuhr, *The Responsible Self* (New York: Harper & Row, 1963), pp. 114–115.

3. See Richard Fox's comment that suicide "is the most significant of all deaths in its impact on survivors, causing long-lasting grief and guilt and a high suicide-expectancy," in A. S. Duncan, G. R. Dunstan, and R. B. Welbourn, eds., *Dictionary of Medical Ethics* (new rev. ed., 1981), p. 426. See also Thomas Wood, "Suicide," in James F. Childress and John Macquarrie, eds., *The Westminster Dictionary of Christian Ethics* (Philadelphia: Westminster Press, 1986), p. 609.

4. Dietrich Bonhoeffer, *Ethics* (New York: Macmillan Co., 1955 [1949]), p. 167.

5. Karl Barth, *Church Dogmatics,* III/4 (Edinburgh: T. & T. Clark, 1961), p. 404.

6. J. Philip Wogaman, *A Christian Method of Moral Judgment* (Philadelphia: Westminster Press, 1976), pp. 74–75.

7. Quoted by Paul W. Pretzel, "Philosophical and Ethical Considerations of Suicide Prevention," in Robert W. Weir, ed., *Ethical Issues in Death and Dying* (New York: Columbia University Press, 1977), p. 388.

8. Mary Rose Barrington, "Apologia for Suicide," in M. Pabst Battin and David J. Mayo, eds., *Suicide: The Philosophical Issues* (New York: St. Martin's Press, 1980), p. 93.

9. Jerome A. Motto, "The Right to Suicide: A Psychiatrist's View" in Battin and Mayo, eds., *Suicide,* pp. 213–217.

10. I remember with great appreciation an elderly woman in a congregation I served as pastor in the 1950s. She was dying of cancer, and I was delegated by the family to inform her. She broke through my awkward words with a smile and the observation that "until the Lord places his hand on my shoulder, I have my work to do here." In spite of her frailty, weakness, and pain she was indeed able to do her "work"—which was to help hold her family together in love.

11. Seneca, "On Suicide," in Robert N. Beck and John B. Orr, *Ethical Choice: A Case Study Approach* (New York: Free Press, 1970), p. 54.

12. Ibid., pp. 54–55.

13. This is by no means limited to the traditional Japanese samurai practices. Western cultures have sometimes tacitly encouraged it, sometimes with tragic results. It appears, for instance, that composer Peter Ilich Tchaikovsky may have been

forced to commit suicide in order to avoid disgrace for homo-sexual behavior.

14. See Karen Lebacqz and H. Tristram Engelhardt, Jr., "Suicide and Covenant," in Battin and Mayo, eds., *Suicide,* p. 86. Lebacqz and Engelhardt do not advocate this practice, and they are clear that such an act must also keep faith with the other covenants to which those who engage in the suicide pact must also be responsible.

15. It may also mean that the larger society has failed in its responsibility to undergird the family, but the larger society often *does* fail at exactly that point. And changing the practices of society is not an option for the one contemplating suicide!

16. Thomas S. Szasz, "The Ethics of Suicide," in Battin and Mayo, eds., *Suicide,* p. 194.

17. Ibid., pp. 193–194.

18. Motto, "The Right to Suicide," p. 218.

19. In a study for the Joint Economic Committee of the U.S. Congress, M. Harvey Brenner discovered that each 1 percent increase in the unemployment rate increased the suicide rate by 4.1 percent. See M. Harvey Brenner, *Estimating the Social Cost of National Economic Policy* (Washington, D.C.: U.S. Congress, Joint Economic Committee, 1976).

20. See A. Alvarez, "The Background," in Battin and Mayo, eds., *Suicide,* pp. 7–32. Reprinted from *The Savage God: A Study of Suicide* (New York: Random House, Bantam Books, 1973).

6

Pastoral Care Perspectives
A. Morgan Parker, Jr.

MORGAN PARKER, currently serving as pastor of the newly chartered San Luis Rey Valley United Methodist Church of Oceanside, California, is also actively speaking and writing on the subject of suicide. He holds a B.A. from UCLA, did his seminary training at Boston University School of Theology, and earned his D.Min. from Wesley Theological Seminary.

His work in the field of suicidology began with doctoral research at the National Institute of Mental Health and Wesley Theological Seminary. For nearly twenty-five years he served as an active-duty navy chaplain, with special assignments in naval hospitals working with suicidal individuals.

Parker's writings include two books, *Suicide Among Young Adults* and *Psalms from the Sea,* in addition to devotional materials and magazine and journal articles. He is an avid tennis player and recommends it as excellent therapy for virtually every affliction of body, mind, or soul.

Traditions, convictions, theological foundations, and ethical determinations have obviously provided a varied basis for considerations of suicide, even as in many other areas of vital belief and decision. The perspective embraced and shared here stems from classic Judeo-Christian convictions regarding the value of purposive human life created by God as delineated in holy scriptures.

Life is a beautiful gift from God. More than that, it is a preciously sacred gift. Human life is framed in the very image of God. "Then God said, 'Let us make man in our image, after our likeness' " (Gen 1:26). The essence of that image or likeness may be endlessly explored, but the person of faith can little doubt the ultimate sanctity of human life.

Scriptures and our faith make clear that we not only come from God but belong to God. We are not our own but have been bought with a price. For Christians, the price is revealed in the self-giving of Christ himself. And in receiving the Christ, we acknowledge our own giving of self to God who is the author, creator, and sustainer of our lives. The faith experience leads us to declare with Paul in Galatians 2:20, "I have been crucified with Christ; it is no longer I who live, but Christ who lives in me." The Christ who lives in me elevates human life and spirit to the Divine from where it came, through which it is sustained, and to which it is destined to return.

The provider of pastoral care, especially in the Christian tradition, is therefore committed to caring intently for the welfare and preservation of this divinely given and divinely filled pinnacle of the Lord's creation. Is this to imply denial of one's right to die? Not at all. This classic Christian conviction says nothing about requiring artificial or mechanical devices to prolong forced existence far beyond the body's natural conclusion to this earthly pilgrimage. But neither is it to assert that either pain or pronouncement of terminal illness is reason to justify removal of respirator or sustenance. Meaningful life is supported, even under greatest strain, as an earthen vessel capable of divine reflection.

The Caring Pastor

The perspective herein considered thus depicts pastoral care as committed to highest reverence for human life, focused on the conviction that life is from and for God, and concerned that every instrument of compassionate regard be employed to sustain enriched, productive human life. This perspective prompts an in-depth study of the dynamics underlying self-destructive behavior as well as an intense commitment to turning the tide toward enriched, self-fulfilling, abundant life.

This is no small task. It will call from the pastoral care provider all the resources, dedication, and empathy humanly possible. It will call for a depth of concern and commitment to service as perhaps never experienced. Only the abiding grace of God can provide resources for such endeavors. May no less than God's grace be fully with those who undertake ministry to persons crying for help, often as the unresponsive crowd passes by.

Gale was one of those crying out. She was a nineteen-year-old English girl whose tragic saga has been movingly portrayed by the BBC. Like many another, hers is the heartrending tale of a young child who spent her growing years in institutions, foster homes, and protective custody. She displayed a range of self-destructive characteristics, from fearful, rebellious, uncooperative, disruptive behavior to heavy drug usage and suicidal intentions.

The final moments of the film *Gale Is Dead* are most revealing. Her one caring friend, a former teacher and the mother of the family with whom she'd stayed, has exhausted her energies and efforts to rehabilitate this young woman. The emaciated teenager is reduced to street life in the vicinity of Piccadilly Circus, surrounded only by drug abusers, pushers, and an uncaring public. She lives in public restrooms, is a stranger to nourishment, and develops symptoms of total physical collapse.

The last retreat of this sad child is to a squalid room where even her final befriender, the former teacher, is unable to communicate with her. Left to her last lonely thoughts, Gale only despairs of life and yearns to die, which she perceives as release. Following an intentional massive drug overdose her contorted, listless body is discovered by the landlord, and her funeral is the capstone lesson in pastoral care for the viewer. The impersonal, aloof, unmoved character of the canned ritual is the final rebuff for this tragic child of God. It serves as the ultimate indignity in a life filled with only tragic heartaches and apathetic indifference.

Hearing the Cry for Help

The oft-repeated phrase, "It's the care that cures," is never more applicable than when we speak of suicidal individuals.

And pastoral care is possibly the most critically needed kind of care at such moments, while its lack or perversion may be literally lethal. The essential question for pastoral care providers is, "Do we really care?"

A development seminar focusing on ethics brought this matter into focus. Chaplains were being led in various group processes by three distinguished resource persons, of Roman Catholic, Protestant, and Jewish faiths. One role-playing scenario depicted a hospital chaplain dealing with a suicidal individual. The patient was a retiree who, in addition to direct expression of suicidal intention, described experiences of loneliness, depression, and declining interest in all activities. Chaplain and patient were interrupted by a passing friend who exchanged greetings with the patient. Shortly after resuming their conversation, the hospital administrator stopped by with additional greetings and jovial comments. Finally, the chaplain noticed the lateness of the hour and began to bid the patient a pleasant evening and God's blessings as another appointment prompted a hasty farewell.

When chaplains participating in the role play were asked to discuss ethical issues as they saw them in this scene, they reported the central issue to be one of confidentiality. And one could tell they took considerable pride in their demonstrated ability to keep the old man's intentions close to the vest. Resource leaders, however, were forthright in declaring confidentiality not at all the crucial concern at this point. The chaplain's chief concern, they reiterated, should have been to exert every effort to minister to the retiree by listening, responding emphatically, and offering personal and other professional counseling assistance. The overwhelming impact of the scene, as portrayed, was that the chaplain really wasn't hearing this man's cry for help and did not care enough to extend himself beyond the most routine of exchanges in dealing with the matter.

The theme is continual. It's the care that cures. Do we really, really care? And if pastors don't, who will? As pastors we need to care, to understand interpersonal dynamics, to have counseling tools and be able to employ them, and to have concern enough to continue employing them.

In the darkness and confusion of our days, few people really care and few are "care" providers. Why should they be? If we operate on a "grab the gusto" philosophy, it makes little sense to risk our time, much less our hides, for others. Only those who have authentically heard and marched to another tune will be capable of caring in full measure. Pastoral care of suicidal individuals comes effectively only from those whose encounter with God's unmerited grace in their lives has turned them in profound gratitude to self-giving for others. We are talking of conversion, deep religious experience, and committed service to God and all God's children for the lifesaving grace God has brought into our lives. Those who are thus prepared can touch and assist in turning the lives of others. Gratitude, service, and self-giving are life-validating experiences that are contagious and truly lifesaving.

Being Available

What are the signs of caring? One is availability. Is the pastor's telephone a means of communication or an impediment to contact? Pastors may not be the easiest people to reach. Messages left with secretaries and even calls to home may all fail. These are matters not to be taken lightly. Somehow the system, or lack of one, must be overcome if pastors are to be effective care providers.

This is a matter of perspective and priorities. Chaplain Harold Mengis, a dynamic navy chaplain, once preached a sermon with a most intriguing title, "The Ministry of Interruptions." This, in a phrase, is the real ministry of the caring pastor. It surely was the ministry of Jesus. And it is surely the ministry required of God's servants who would dedicate themselves to saving the lost and dying. To reach the isolated and alienated, one must hear the cry, be willing to modify an agenda, and offer deep personal care.

Paul Tournier shows the desperate need for such when he says:

> Above all it is personal relationship which is tragically lacking in
> a world of power in which men are entirely preoccupied with ful-

filling their function, with playing their part in the great economic machine which has tamed them so thoroughly. . . . It seems to me that is what the young are seeking so ardently when they come together in their small groups, often without saying anything, without doing anything, down in a cellar, listening to a pop record: A tremendous need for human fellowship.[1]

The pastor represents and communicates a personal relationship, a fellowship beyond even the human plane. His or hers is the privilege of bringing people to a relationship with the One who will never leave them alone or comfortless. This is a spiritual blessing of immeasurable value. Again Tournier says:

In my view it is just this spiritual dimension that our civilization has left in the shadow, or at least in the twilight. It includes all that is irrational in man: his need for beauty, for poetry, for mystery and dreams, his need for love, for personal contact with others, with nature, and with God.[2]

This loss of contact may be the factor that pushes the desperate, lonely, or depressed toward self-destruction. Their cry for help all too often is totally unheeded amid the pressing throng. They do cry, call, and reach out, even if in sometimes veiled language. This is why John Naisbitt says we vitally need the counterbalancing human response, *high touch* to match our high tech! The lack of contact through personal touch is no doubt behind the spiraling suicide rates of our time. *Focus on the Family* magazine reported that over 5,000 teenagers commit suicide every year, and for each of these another 50 to 100 attempt suicide.[3] For the young adult between 17 and 25, suicide remains the second highest cause of death following accidents—many of which could in turn be generated by self-destructive motives.

Understanding the Problem

It is imperative to remember that we face the would-be suicidal person daily. The season for caring and prevention is always now, and to accomplish that we need to keep ever before us some basic understandings about suicide.

While patterns are shifting to some degree, evidence still points to certain high probabilities regarding the suicidal individual. Approximately four times as many men as women actually take their own lives. In our culture, white males have highest rates and young adult black males show the highest percent of increase. Protestants are reported to take their own lives seven times more frequently than Catholics. Ancient church laws, theological positions, and social cohesiveness tend to account for these wide differences. Ninety percent of all who actually die of suicide do so by one of three methods— shooting, stabbing, or hanging.

April is considered the cruelest month of the year, with more people dying in spring or on holidays than at any other time. Researchers indicate people seem unable to tolerate the contrasts. Stability is possible when the rest of the world is cold, drab, and despondent along with the suicidal. But the contrast of colorful flowers, budding life, or jovial seasons is too much.

Understanding such characteristics can better prepare one to appreciate the lethality of the case at hand, that one may respond appropriately. Respond is the key word: Shneidman and Farberow in their classic *Cry for Help* have well documented the need to respond.[4] Their thesis is that all suicidal activity is indeed a cry for help. No one wants to die, they say. The hope is that someone will really hear and respond.

To do so effectively one must hear the clues, sometimes veiled and sometimes clearly broadcast. Many people will be open and direct, with blunt statements, often repeated, of how they simply want to die. Bystanders will frequently ignore such words entirely or pass them off lightly, saying, "Now, you don't mean that," or "You'll feel different later—just keep going."

Instead, the care provider needs to say, "Hey, what's going on with you?" or "Want to talk about it?" A genuinely attentive and empathetic listener can literally save a life. The crisis hot-line people tell us twenty minutes is the length of the average lifesaving conversation. That amount of caring time can release burdens, turn around despair, and open avenues to other options. Some experiments suggest that actual brain processes are somehow momentarily irregular in the suicidal person. Evidence points to sudden extremeness and rigidity not often characteristic of a particular individual. This appears to be accompanied by actual changes temporarily taking place in body and brain chemistry. Providing the brief time needed for these unusual thought patterns to correct themselves can make all the difference.

Of course, many clues from the distraught person may not be as direct. Giving away prized possessions, canceling all memberships, and giving up all positions and responsibilities would be important signals of a self-destructive drive. A radical change of personal habits or daily routine, involving activities such as eating, sleeping, and drug or alcohol usage should be explored as possibly significant indicators.

Responding with Compassion

Most critical is the quality of personal relationships. Strong, meaningful, empathetic, and loving relationships will carry distressed persons through the darkest moments. Strained, uncaring, destructive relationships will be found after the fact of suicide in nearly all situations. The presence of a "primary significant other" who really cares, responds, and continues compassionately reaching out is the principal lifesaving ingredient for suicidal persons.

One organization, the Befrienders of Boston, has achieved considerable success in its ability to hear by phone and respond with understanding akin to a primary significant other. The organization has published descriptive lists of signs to help befrienders evaluate lethality and pointers to guide their response. These materials, as presented here, should prove invaluable to the pastor who would assist the suicidal individual.[5]

Signs of Depression and Suicide Risk

Sadness, withdrawal
Lack of interest in activities previously enjoyed
Apathy and fatigue
Pessimism, irritability
Loss of appetite and weight
Loss of sexual interest

Sleep disturbance, insomnia, or early waking
  nightmares
Difficulty in making conversation and carrying out
  routine tasks
Sense of futility
Indecisiveness
Feelings of worthlessness
Loss of religious faith
Feelings of guilt and self-blame
Preoccupation with illness, real or imaginary
Financial worries
Drug or alcohol dependence
Preoccupation with or talk about suicide
A definite plan for committing suicide
Suicidal impulses
Previous suicide attempts
Social isolation
Recent loss
No hope for the future
Unsympathetic relatives, a feeling that nobody cares
Tidying up affairs, giving away possessions
Suicides in the family or among close friends
Fear of losing control, going crazy, harming self
  or others
Feelings of helplessness
Low energy
Anxiety
Stress

Often people are most at risk when they seem to be improving. Sometimes when a person has contemplated suicide for a long time, even a seemingly trivial mental stress can set off a tragedy.

If a person seems depressed, don't be afraid to ask, "Do you feel badly enough to kill yourself?" It can be a great relief if you bring up the subject and let the person talk freely about suicidal thoughts, feelings, impulses, plans, fantasies. Talking about it to someone who is accepting, who doesn't show shock or disapproval, can clear the air and reduce the tension. Nearly everyone can be helped to overcome almost any kind of situation if there is someone who will listen, take the conversation seriously, and show that he or she cares. Again, the Befrienders provide valuable assistance in this task.

Pointers for Befriending Suicidal or Despairing People

1. All befriending is played by ear. There are no formulas, just safe guidelines.
2. You must *be yourself.* Anything else feels phony, sounds phony, and won't seem natural to you or to the person who is talking with you.
3. Your job is to make a relationship so the other person feels he or she can trust you enough to tell you what the problem really is. You want the person to be able to level with you as if you were a good friend.
4. What you say or don't say is not as important as how you say it. If you can't find the right words but feel genuine concern, your voice and manner will convey this.
5. Deal with the person, not just the problem. Talk as an equal; if you try to act like a counselor or an expert or try to solve problems, it will probably be resented.
6. Give your full attention. Listen for feelings as well as facts, and for what is *not* said as well as what is said. Allow the person to unburden without interruption.
7. Don't feel you have to say something every time there is a pause. Silence gives each of you time to think.
8. Show interest and invite the person to continue without giving him or her the third degree. Simple, direct questions ("What happened?" "What's the matter?") are less threatening than complicated, probing ones.
9. Steer toward the pain, not away from it. The person wants to tell you about private, painful things that most other people don't want to hear. Sometimes you have to provide an opening and give permission to begin talking. ("You sound depressed. What's the matter?")
10. Try to see and feel things from the other person's point of view. Be on his or her side; don't side with people he or she may be hurting or being hurt by.

11. Let the person find answers, even if you think you see an obvious solution.
12. Many times there are no answers, and your role is to bear witness, to listen, to be with the person. Giving your time, attention, and concern may not seem like doing enough. People in distress, in seemingly hopeless situations, can make you feel helpless and inadequate. Happily, you do not have to come up with solutions or change people's lives, or even save their lives. They will save themselves and make their own changes. Trust them. WHEN YOU DON'T KNOW WHAT TO SAY, SAY NOTHING.

The Caring Community

The greatest help for someone in distress may come from a genuinely caring community. Caring communities come in many forms. A knowledgeable circle of friends, an extended family, or a club, team, fraternal organization, or local church may all qualify. Whenever warm, honest, supportive concern for one another is found, there in the midst will be lifesaving power. Entire towns and cities may exhibit either a friendly, outgoing concern for the neighbor or an aloof, detached anonymity that isolates and devastates.

Is this behind some of the geographical divergences in suicide occurrence figures? We're told if you want to live in a suicide-free environment, move to South Carolina or Alabama or Louisiana. The Southeast has the lowest suicide rate in the country, while the mobile, swinging West Coast states have the highest. Is there something about community stability reflected in these figures that points to effects in individual lives?

The caring community in which support, empathy, and compassion may be experienced needs to be reliable, stable, and outgoing in human exchanges. The revolving-door characteristic of most contemporary American society places a real strain on efforts to know and care about one another.

Obviously, the church is not immune from our transient syndrome. Many persons exhibit the short-timer's attitude as shown by their making little effort or having little desire to know or care about those whom they estimate will be present only briefly. So prevalent is this sense of transiency that one can hardly assume a caring community will spontaneously occur in our society. The pastoral care provider, then, sees the building of a caring community as central to ministry to suicidal persons.

How one goes about such a task has limitless possibilities, yet all are related to building warm, honest, caring relationships. Helping people to have fun and enjoy one another's company is key. Developing common goals and projects and investing energy together to pursue them is important. An entire community can catch this caring spirit through mutually shared endeavors that accomplish worthy results. One such experience is the CROP walk for Church World Service. Coordinators of these annual events, held across the United States, have had the privilege of seeing people pull together, plan with enthusiasm, and go forth with renewed feelings of self-worth and common purpose. Every community can benefit from such efforts.

A caring community can develop among care providers who see the value to themselves and their people multiplied. Such was the case at the U.S. Military Academy according to U'ren, Conrad, and Patterson in a 1970–71 study.[6] Their paper demonstrated how coordinated, mutually caring services by the mental hygiene consultation service, counseling office, and chaplain's office apparently contributed to preventing a considerable number of suicides.

Perhaps no informal, civic, or professional community can equal the effective caring found in the church that is truly a dedicated, intentional, caring community. Opening avenues to God while bestowing God's affection through outstretched human arms is unquestionably life-affirming, redeeming, and saving. Another research study seems to document this conviction. Terry Parsons and Bernard Alger examined 98 intentional drug overdose patients admitted to Presbyterian Hospital of Dallas from June 15, 1972, to April 24, 1973.[7] Only seven considered themselves active church members. One may well infer that strong, active church life would not be characteristic of the vast majority of persons resorting to suicide attempts.

Another message from Parsons and Alger supports the link to community offered by hospital chaplains. They say that "since most of these patients were not actively involved in a local church congregation," the chaplain would supply supportive transitional care until alternative referral arrangements could be established. This could involve, as they prescribe, follow-up calls to the person after his or her discharge from the hospital. The caring community is one that will reach out.

One case in point concerned an elderly female patient on the medical ward of the naval hospital at Camp Pendleton. She emphatically refused her lunch tray, just as the hospital chaplain was coming to be with her. The chaplain could tell something beyond the particular menu offering was of concern to her. When he inquired about her response, she said, "Chaplain, these people are on a different program from mine." He asked about her program, and she replied, "All I want is to have my ashes scattered at sea like my husband's were three months ago." She continued as a hostile, uncooperative patient till the day of her discharge to a nearby nursing home several days later. But before she left, the chaplain had become sufficiently well acquainted to learn of her beautiful family and to emphasize her value for her daughter and grandchildren. He followed up with a letter to the nursing home, suggesting a time together if she would accept such a visit. She called shortly thereafter and they had some meaningful talks. She transferred to another home farther away, but their correspondence continued, and so far as the chaplain knows, she's alive now with a newfound source of inner strength and outer joy in relationships with her family.

The caring must go on if life is to go on. Only the care that reaches out even beyond institutional doors and parish boundaries will be effective in the final analysis. Such care should be extended to suicidal individuals, their families, and, if need be, their survivors.

Caring for Survivors

Sad to say, the call for supportive ministry comes more and more frequently from those who are the survivors of suicide's tragedy. With ever increasing rates of occurrence of suicide for persons of all ages, it follows that pastoral care providers find themselves receiving many calls for assistance and comfort. Seldom will they minister to persons in deeper grief, shock, and trauma. The loss of dearest friends or loved ones in what seems to be needless death is both stunning and deeply distressing.

To such shock and grief the pastoral care provider brings resources available nowhere else. To hear that God is still powerfully present with understanding compassion and hope amid encircling gloom is very likely the margin of difference for healing so terribly wounded a soul. That assurance is likely to be best communicated through the earthen vessel of a truly empathetic pastoral ministry. Such ministry incorporates both the essentials of deep compassion and the confidence of rational meaning behind some agonizing variables of the universe. These essentials are communicated best in simple ways. In quietness will be our strength. Calm presence speaks powerfully. Those who believe fervently in the indwelling Christ bring not only themselves but the focused presence of God's continuing incarnation. That incarnation imparts the message of life over death. It affirms that though we die, yet shall we live. No greater comfort or consolation can be offered the grieving heart that is suffering the loss of a loved one.

The calming influence of this divine support will go far, as well, to stem what is often considered unexplainable multiple tragedies. Reports are many of one high school student after another repeating the horror of self-inflicted disaster. Much of this chain-reaction response is a mystery, to be sure, and may ever remain so. Yet it is highly possible that much emotional volatile reaction could be precluded by the empathetic, assuring calm of pastoral care support. Lack of such calming and sustaining ministry, early on, may well be a favor in other elements having their devastating result.

Even as certain group dynamics may harm an individual, when unchecked, so may the gracious cycle of a sustaining fellowship be uplifting. Pastoral care may reach its most effective point well after the hour of crisis. Weeks and months later, a grieving person may find the referred fellowship group to be of invaluable assistance. Support groups may take the form of church youth fellowships, caring Bible study classes, prayer groups, men's and women's organizations, and virtually the whole range of experiences where the gathered community may extend the love of God through God's caring servants.

This gathered community might well be the distinct opportunity for a bereaved person to discover deepest fulfillment through prayer and quiet reflective moments with God. Both prayer for one another and broader prayer concerns could lift one beyond the personal crisis at hand to the broader avenues of life and service to others. By this process a fractured, hurting child of God might come again to the poise of self-giving perspective.

Only then may one open again the windows to continued life and enrichment. Only then may the hurting heart turned within become the restored spirit inspired to move outward. Many prayers will be truly answered, as a recovering servant embraces anew the way of faith and, out of the crucible of shattering experience, offers compassionate understanding to others.

Outreach

Much of the pain in pastoral care comes with awareness of the many who seek no such support before, during, or after deep crisis. How may the pastor more effectively reach isolated, alienated persons hurting alone on every street? The very question may be immobilizing. For no pastor or designated counselor can singly discern and lead the many who hurt to springs of healing and comfort. The pastor's task, therefore, may well be to serve as catalyst in mobilizing others to reach out or be responsive to cries of the alienated. To speak in these terms is to think far more seriously about developing a wide sense of community caring. This is a caring which, while respectful of privacy, is willing at some point to risk involvement where the open, festering hurt is painfully obvious.

To call for this kind of caring community is to call for perhaps no less than a major refocusing of society. The pride we've so ardently embraced in one individual's single-handed achievements may need to be tempered by heightened community identity and responsibility. If we have been able to discover how to build better automobiles through cooperative group responsibility and teamwork, should we not be able to do the same in working together to enrich and sustain one another in daily living? We already have a number of exemplary models in specialized endeavors such as athletics. The enthusiasm and renewed community spirit often displayed for a winning home team is a vast potential with which zest for life's other important concerns could also be upheld. The land of the free need not mean we freely choose to isolate ourselves; it can also be a freedom for investing ourselves in common causes. The art of team building is essential for neighborhood and community building in our time.

Granted, the challenge is not made easier by the nature of contemporary American society. Our immense diversity seems only to continue. Our language, racial, and cultural differences are extremely complex. The typical family today is far different from the neighborhood family of yesteryear. Single-parent homes, unmarried adults living together or in isolation, the growing older population—all call for creative new understandings of community.

The pastoral care provider and the church have significant contributions to make in facing this creative challenge. We proclaim a God who is one and who calls us into a unity of oneness. Across every boundary, barrier, or border, we are called to see all people as equal sons and daughters of this compassionate God. We can and should be at the very forefront of community endeavors to respect and cherish each member as precious. This is the foundation for genuine community caring. It is the motivation that can mold us together, holding one another with our precious values and enriched life, as a common cause.

The isolated and alienated can thus know both the compassion of an accepting God and the support of an inclusive community. This assures the continued presence of the "primary significant other" who is essential in sustaining life. Both the sanctity of life and the enrichment of it through human acceptance provides hope for finally turning the tide against suicide.

Conclusion

Pastoral care, undergirded by the grace of God and dedicated to upholding life as a precious gift of God, is thus uniquely capable of bringing great insight and assistance to the suicidal individual. When the pastoral care provider understands the basic dynamics of suicidal behavior, is committed to responding to cries for help, and mobilizes others to be effective instruments of caring, then healing, by God's grace, is near at hand. The gift of life abundant may thus be shared, sustained, and dedicated to serving God and the people of God.

NOTES

1. Paul Tournier, *The Violence Within* (New York: Harper & Row, 1978), p. 191.

2. Ibid., p. 121.

3. David Elkind, *Focus on the Family* (April 1985), pp. 2–4.

4. Norman L. Farberow and Edwin S. Shneidman, eds., *Cry for Help* (New York: McGraw-Hill Book Co., 1961).

5. Used by permission of Befrienders of Boston, Samaritans, 500 Commonwealth Avenue, Kenmore Square, Boston, Mass. 02215.

6. Richard C. U'ren, Francis E. Conrad, and Peter H. Patterson, "A Year's Experience in Student Mental Health at West Point," *American Journal of Psychiatry* 130(6):643–647 (June 1973).

7. Terry Parsons and Bernard C. Alger, "Characteristics of Drug Overdosed Patients and Supplementary Treatment Needs," *Journal of Pastoral Care* 33(2):88–95 (1979).

7

A Process Perspective
Robert L. Kinast

ROBERT L. KINAST is a priest of the Archdiocese of Atlanta. After completing seminary studies at the Pontifical College Josephinum, he was ordained in 1968 and served a number of parishes until 1977. During his time in Atlanta, he earned a Ph.D. in systematic theology at Emory University.

Kinast began teaching pastoral theology at The Catholic University of America in 1977. He has lectured widely in the United States, has published over forty articles in pastoral and theological journals, and has written four books: *When a Person Dies, Caring for Society, From Cell to Society* (with Dr. Judith Schloegel), and *Sacramental Pastoral Care.*

Since 1985 Kinast has taught pastoral theology at the Washington Theological Union in Silver Spring, Maryland. He is a theologian consultant to the Catholic Bishops Committee on the Laity and has helped design an adult learning-action program for the National Pastoral Life Center.

Rich was unable to feel good about himself. His business kept losing money until he had to file for bankruptcy, he distanced himself emotionally from his wife and children, and he began to drink excessively. Finally, one night he took his handgun and shot himself to death. In the note he left behind, he apologized to everyone he loved and asked them to understand that he just didn't want to burden their lives any longer.

Gloria was 70 and for the last five years had been living in a home for the elderly. She had never married and had no immediate family. When she was diagnosed as having a terminal illness that would require extensive and uncomfortable treatments, she must have decided to end her life by taking an overdose of drugs. She was found alone in her bed with no final message or explanation.

Karen was a bright, talented teenager, active in school and an honor student. She seemed to succeed at any task and almost automatically was given leadership roles. One day she went home, locked herself in the garage, and started the car's engine. Her family, friends, and neighbors were stunned, especially when they found a letter from her saying that she felt people respected her only for her intelligence or her skill but not for who she was.

Lee was a native of southeast Asia. He escaped from his country and emigrated to the United States. He was very active in trying to publicize conditions in his country, and he lobbied full-time for financial and diplomatic aid. One day in a city park he set himself on fire to dramatize the destruction of human life that his words had not succeeded in conveying.

These are four cases of suicide, and yet each one is quite different. The motive, the circumstances, and the intended effect vary from one case to the next, and yet the term "suicide" covers them all. This is a reminder that a single term that covers such different situations should be used with care. At the same time, the variety of these cases helps to identify those characteristics common to suicide that recur despite the many variables. Three general characteristics appear here.

First, the act is self-directed. This, of course, is the literal meaning of *sui*-cide. But Rich, Gloria, Karen, and Lee are not simply or entirely alone. Each is part of a network of other people and events, even if that network is not very meaningful (as in Karen's case) or supportive (as in Lee's case). So to say suicide is self-directed is not to say a person is living or acting in isolation, even if that is what the person feels.

Second, every suicide terminates the life of that person. This, of course, is the essential meaning of death, whatever its form, but death that is self-directed is especially poignant because it *is* self-directed. Death ordinarily results from forces outside our control. So even the most shocking or illogical death is understandable because it verifies the instinct that all of us are vulnerable and live threatened existences. But we do live, despite the risk and danger. Suicide contradicts that impulse and puts death on another plane—the threat from within.

Third, suicide has an unsettling effect on survivors that other death experiences do not seem to have. At its core this is because we feel that death isn't supposed to originate from within. Our inner impulse is supposed to be toward living, overcoming obstacles, pushing on. When this doesn't happen, it is troubling.

This feeling is often expressed by our surprise that someone like Gloria even considered suicide, much less carried it out. Accompanying the surprise is often a sense of responsibility, if not culpability, for not anticipating and preventing the suicide, as in the case of Rich. At a deeper level, however, suicide is a reminder that all of us have the same potential to reverse the thrust toward living and terminate our own lives. In fact, suicide may even recall times when we ourselves considered doing just that very thing.

These common characteristics take suicide out of the realm of the merely particular or personal or unique, where it might be easily avoided, and puts it in the realm of shared human experience. In this realm we are able to examine the phenomenon of suicide from many perspectives and try to gain a clearer understanding of both suicide and human living.

I want to use the perspective of process thought here to reflect on suicide. Process thought is an intriguing perspective because its stress on becoming seems to be the antithesis of what suicide represents. However, a closer examination shows that process thought is very congenial to the common characteristics just mentioned, but its way of understanding these characteristics reveals a view of life in which suicide is not compatible. To see what this means, I will reflect on the three common characteristics of suicide from the perspective of Alfred North Whitehead, one of the originators of process thought.[1]

Self-Direction

One of the distinctive features of a process worldview is that the things that ultimately make up the world are self-directed.[2] To understand what this means, it is necessary to see the world through process eyes. The world is composed of innumerable momentary events called "actual occasions" or "actual entities." The key word is "actual." It signifies that the events that make up the world are active; they are in the process of becoming what they will be. This is true of the minute energy impulses of atoms and molecules, of the complex behavior of cells, of the intricate coordination of plant and animal life, of the unique mental activity of human beings, and of the all-embracing experience of God.

The process of becoming consists of three basic phases.[3] First, there is an initial aim that draws an event into action. The initial aim arises from the previous occasions of experience from which the present occasion emerges. For example, Rich's drinking emerged when his business went bankrupt; Lee's lobbying efforts arose from his escape to the United States.

But initial aims do not arise on their own. They are first grasped and then presented to us by God. Thus God is the originator of all new events in the universe.[4] God does this by taking in the whole experience that has just occurred and immediately sensing the next best possibilities for becoming (e.g., for Karen or Gloria). God's experience is to feel with the whole creation what it has just become in each of its actual occasions. Out of this feeling God draws all the possible aims and initiates the next phase of becoming by conveying these aims with a feeling of desire or attraction corresponding to their value in God's sight. For example, after Rich's business failed, God may have seen Rich's relationship with his family as the most valuable aim and his excessive drinking as the least valuable.

The second phase of becoming is the actualizing of the aim. This is the self-directed part. Each event comes into being out of the stream of events of its immediate past, senses the aim God proposes, and responds to that aim more or less successfully.

The response of each event consists in the way that event

feels, or takes in from the world available to it, those elements that will satisfy the initial aim. For example, Gloria receives the news about her illness. God's aim is, let us say, that she share this news and her feelings with others so she will enjoy their support. She may do this, or she may sense another possible aim—bear it alone—and respond to that aim instead.

Human beings almost always sense several possible aims for their becoming. Along with these aims, there are many ways in which any one of them might be satisfied. For example, Karen may want to feel appreciated as a person. She has many opportunities and many resources for actualizing this aim, but it may require more initiative on her part than she is willing or able to put forth. Because human beings have a range of possibilities and a variety of resources for satisfying them, the actual experience of human becoming fluctuates a great deal.

The third phase of becoming occurs once an event is completed. As soon as this happens, it is available for inclusion in new events. Usually these are the very next moments in a series.[5] For example, Lee talks to one senator about the plight of his homeland, and when that conversation is completed he talks to another senator. The second conversation includes the experience of the first conversation, as well as other factors (e.g., this is the second time Lee has spoken to this senator; Lee is growing increasingly frustrated because conditions in his homeland have worsened).

In general, what one event makes available for the next event is the feeling that arises from having satisfied the aim of that event, more or less well. For example, Gloria fights off her tendency to bear it alone and shares herself with other residents in the home. This generates a feeling of togetherness rather than isolation. This feeling is taken up by God, harmonized with all the other relevant feelings about Gloria, and offered back to her for new experiences of becoming.

On the other hand, Rich resists sharing his feelings with his family and turns to alcohol instead. His action generates an experience of distancing rather than intimacy. As God takes in this experience, it doesn't allow for much of a change in Rich's becoming. God is limited in this case because the best aims God can offer are drawn from Rich's self-directed experience.

Sometimes the best is not very good; sometimes it is not very attractive. The whole process of becoming is an adventure for both God and the events that make up the world.

If we look at suicide from this perspective, we can say the following. Suicide, like all actual events, is self-directed. It is, moreover, a response to aims that are felt with varying degrees of attraction by the person. Perhaps Karen feels there is no other way to get people to see her as a person. Perhaps Gloria feels this is the best way to avoid painful treatments.

Since all aims come from God, it may be said that the possibility of suicide originates with God. But its value in God's view is another matter. In general we would say that suicide is at the low end of the spectrum from God's point of view, for reasons that will be made clear when discussing the third common characteristic. But from the point of view of a depressed person like Rich, or someone like Gloria who has lived a long life and doesn't want to face painful treatments, suicide can have a high appeal and even supplant other aims that God senses are preferable.

The human capacity for self-direction is very strong and is intensified by the influence of a person's past, especially the immediate past. As with all processes of becoming, human becoming arises out of the experience of its own past. The past always inclines the next occasion to repeat what has just occurred. If the immediately past experience has been disappointing (as with Karen) or frustrating (as with Lee), it conditions the next experience to conform to that feeling and to reenact it in the next moment of becoming. Thus patterns are formed that are increasingly difficult to alter or reverse.

The effect is to exclude new possibilities and to reduce the range of creativity. For human beings this is analogous to what we call death, when our becoming ceases and the possibility of new experience is ended. The more Rich or Gloria or Karen or Lee reenact experiences with this feeling, the more like death their lives become and the greater the appeal to actualize what they are feeling by ending their lives.

The human capacity for self-direction is the glory and adventure of human becoming that we rightly judge to be superior to the capacity of any other creature we know. But it requires of each person a comparable degree of self-direction and selection from all the options confronting us at any moment. For some people this range of options can be overwhelming and feel threatening (as in Rich's case or Karen's). Others experience extreme disappointment in the choices they see before them, or else they simply don't see any suitable choices (as in Gloria's case). Still others (like Lee) experience frustration as they try to satisfy aims which they sense are the best but which they do not have the resources to accomplish.

Process thought both affirms the self-direction of all becoming and appreciates the peculiar demands this makes on human beings. The affirmation is a form of bonding with the whole universe and all its parts. The appreciation is a recognition of how fragile and tentative human becoming is. This double awareness carries over into a reflection on the other two characteristics of suicide.

Termination

The last phase of every actual event is a completion of the becoming of that event. For example, Rich files for bankruptcy; Gloria hears the diagnosis of her illness. Our lives are composed of a myriad of such events. The continuity we experience is not so much the endurance of a single entity who does different things according to a self-contained human nature (the classic philosophical view). It is the succession of millions of discrete events succeeding each other in a coordinated pattern (the process view). This sequence is described as a perpetual perishing. Human beings are not the only entities that endure in this way, but we are the most interesting because we are conscious of both our endurance and our mortality. The two are always in fierce tension with each other.

To perish, in process terms, is to culminate a momentary enjoyment of becoming. Whatever the quality of experience in that moment (joy, sadness, success, failure, boredom, creativity), it can be available for new acts of becoming only after it is completed. Until it is completed, an event is not actual; it has no definiteness, and therefore it has no value.

Value is determined by two factors, (1) the intrinsic satisfaction enjoyed in the act of becoming and (2) the contribution that experience makes to subsequent acts of becoming. Both factors call for termination of the process. An indefinite process is like a suspended thought; it is nothing until it is complete.

Like the becoming of an event, so too the termination is self-directed in the sense that the event exhausts its potential for satisfying its initial aim. For example, Karen feels unappreciated as a person after being elected class president; Lee feels hopeless after talking with a congressional committee. But immediately the just-completed event yearns for another moment; it already anticipates a new event emerging from its completion. For example, Karen will refuse the election; Lee will meet with the media.

The next moment need not be confined to one's own series of becoming. In fact, some of the most significant events of human becoming are terminated precisely so that others may enjoy the experience as part of their becoming (e.g., works of art, publication of research, closing of contracts).

The life force of the world oscillates between two experiences: the intrinsic enjoyment of one's own becoming and the contribution of that experience to new becoming (one's own or another's). The contribution to one's own becoming is usually stronger because the impact of the immediate previous experience yearns for repetition. This generates a tendency to anticipate one's own continuation after each event and act in ways to ensure that likelihood (by protecting one's well-being, securing the resources for one's needs, seeking the support or affirmation of one's worth). As a person's experiences of continued existence accumulate, the desire for endurance grows, leading eventually to the prospect of continued life in some form after death.[6]

When process thought interprets suicide from this perspective, it acknowledges that the prospect of terminating one's sequence of becoming is not that abnormal and surely not unnatural. We, like all actual entities, end our experience of becoming all the time. But because each experience of perishing gives rise to a new experience of becoming, we tend to focus on the continuation and not the termination. Nonetheless, choosing to end one's life permanently certainly has a different feel to it from the perpetual perishing of process thought that always gives rise to a new experience. The permanence of perishing in suicide is striking because it represents such a tremendous contrast to the ever-deepening hold that continued experiences of becoming have on us. For example, what must it take for Gloria to end her life after seventy years of reinforced experiences of living?

Suicide makes us realize how powerful self-direction is if it can terminate the whole process of becoming in a person. If the motive for this permanent perishing comes from the experience of the intrinsic satisfaction of one's life, it suggests that the person did not enjoy living sufficiently to keep becoming (Rich or Karen). If the motive for this permanent perishing comes from the experience of the contribution of one's life to others, it is more understandable and perhaps even virtuous in the sense that martyrs and heroes are honored (Lee).

The twin perspectives of internal satisfaction and contribution to others are inseparable. What we contribute to others (God and the world) is our own experience of becoming. And ultimately we have neither the internal satisfaction of our experience nor the contribution of that experience to others unless we perish, terminate our acts of becoming, and thereby make them definite, actual events. We terminate our experience for the sake of its contribution to new experience, but we do so seeking the fullest intrinsic satisfaction that the experience can yield. We do each for the sake of the other. This reflection leads to the third characteristic.

Unsettling

Process thought sees the world as interdependent. The whole creative universe arises out of individual actual events, but these events in turn are always derived from the possibilities that the whole creative universe generates. There is no prior self-contained existence of one without the other. There is only a constant process of becoming, which oscillates between the one and the many, the whole and its parts. The connection between single events and the whole creative process is God. It is God alone who takes in all actual events and derives from them the best possibilities for future events, for new acts of becoming.

As just described, the experience of perishing is an integral and necessary part of this process. But to choose and enact a permanent perishing of one's becoming is different. This experience not only seems to run counter to the thrust of life enhancement, it also makes us aware of how much influence we have on the process itself—specifically on God's role in the process and God's way of persuasively luring us toward new life. Rich, Gloria, Karen, and Lee live in a world full of contrasting experiences of depression and vitality, of despair and hope, of pain and healing. They decide which side of the contrasts they will incorporate into their becoming and thereby condition the possibilities for the future and the role of God in initiating it.

It may be objected that relatively few people commit suicide, so the negative effects are not that pervasive. But in process thought there are no simply private events.[7] Every occurrence is public in the sense that it affects the whole creative process. It is a momentary microcosm of what the world can be, based on what it actually is in this particular event. The event of suicide suggests the possibility that the world could permanently perish.

This is what is so unsettling about suicide. It may be tragic for the individual and it may arouse feelings of guilt or missed responsibility in others, but ultimately suicide is a negative statement about God. It says that God couldn't persuade Rich or Gloria or Karen or Lee that the value of their becoming was a contribution to the whole world. It says that God's kind of world isn't worth it, and God's way of creating it is not appealing enough.

This is a severe judgment. It calls into question the very nature of the creative process and reverses the question of judgment that suicide usually raises.[8] Ordinarily, judgment concerns God's verdict about the eternal fate of Rich or Gloria or Karen or Lee and perhaps about those who should have been able to prevent them from committing suicide. But rarely does suicide pronounce judgment on God the way, for example, tragic accidents or fatal events of nature do. Part of the reason for this is that suicide is self-inflicted, and it is presumed that persons have choices and ultimate control that they opt not to exercise. Ultimately, they are responsible, rather than outside forces or *the* outside force, God.

In an interdependent world, however, everything works both ways. We are responsible for our actions, but in response to the initiative of God. And the way God initiates each moment of becoming bears scrutiny in the case of suicide.

In process thought God does not force on us the best possibility for our becoming, nor does God coerce us to keep becoming, even if we are young like Karen or enjoy freedom like Lee. God's style is persuasive, suggestive, appealing to our enjoyment of creative experience, freely assembled. God is like an artist or "the great companion—the fellow sufferer who understands."[9]

This does not mean that God is indifferent to our response. In process thought God is always passionately concerned with our every experience because these actual events are the very stuff from which God's own becoming continues. In every circumstance God invites us to our most satisfying experience, both for our own enjoyment and for God's. God yearns for Rich to pull his life together, for Gloria to experience her dignity, for Karen to feel accepted, for Lee to know success. But God will not compromise our freedom to accomplish this.

We, however, may not only compromise our freedom but negate it in a final act of permanent perishing. If we do so, we say in effect that God was not effective in our regard, that God's persuasiveness didn't work, that ultimately God may not be powerful enough to sustain the universe at this level.

And yet, God persists. No refusal, however misguided or misinformed, can deter God from the way of persuasive appeal. Even the ultimate judgment that is a person's suicide is itself a new event from which God draws the best possibilities and feeds them back into a world that struggles to advance. In some ways this most unsettling aspect of suicide actually enhances God's bountiful fidelity to the process, for God takes in even this event and finds a place for it in the continuing scheme of becoming.[10]

We, who remain the active agents in that continuing process, are likewise confronted by the meaning of a person's suicide. If we turn our attention inward and focus on our feelings of guilt or culpability or remorse, we perpetuate the unsettling impact of the suicide. We allow the power of Rich's depression or Karen's isolation to paralyze our own becoming, and we reinforce those experiences that tend toward permanent perishing rather than the perpetual perishing that is life-giving.

On the other hand, we cannot simply dismiss the suicide of a spouse or friend or family member as if it didn't happen, for we are partly shaped by such experiences. The challenge that suicide poses for us in a process perspective is to get in touch with God's feelings about it, to open ourselves to God's response, and to sense God's creativity, not despite the suicide but including it. How can we do this? God's pattern can be our own.

First of all, God feels with the person who commits suicide. Only by taking in the experience can God draw from it new possibilities. We tend to do this by offering sympathetic explanations of why Gloria or Lee did what they did rather than condemning them. This does not mean glossing over the more disturbing aspects of their actions. It means concentrating on their experience and feeling with the person, not ourselves. If we do the latter, we perpetuate the unsettling effect of suicide, as just mentioned.

Second, God does not withdraw because of suicide but enters more deeply the interdependence with our world. God draws close to us. We too need to be with others, to immerse ourselves in a living network of experiences that allow us to feel the surge and attraction of becoming. We need to tell our stories and hear theirs, to express our feelings and receive theirs. We need to deepen our bonds and affirm our connectedness.

Third, God brings forth the possibility of a new experience. We too need to experience ourselves in a new way with the person who committed suicide. Liturgy and ritual prayer are unique helps in this regard because they allow us to feel the presence of Rich or Karen as the focus of our prayers and attention rather than as someone praying alongside us. We can begin to sense Rich or Karen on the other side of our prayer, where we typically depict God and the holy ones.

This is an experience that opens new possibilities for becoming because we have a new relationship with those who have died. Of course, we may want to hold on to the old way of relating to them (which is no longer possible) and thereby choose an aim other than the most creative one God offers us.

Other experiences serve the same purpose as we share time with Rich's family, recall Gloria's long life, renew Karen's positive effect on us, tell strangers about Lee's commitment. In all these ways we make each person a living part of our own becoming and of the interdependence we create in our experience. In short, they become a source of new experience for us, not a sign of negative experience or of permanent perishing.

None of this is easy. It takes effort, decision, energy, intention. When seen from the perspective of process thought, suicide brings us back to the realization that our becoming, the becoming of the world, and the becoming of God are self-directed. It reminds us that this world is constantly perishing but being reborn in the offer of new life that God gives back to us. And finally it confronts us with the way of divine persuasion—fragile, compassionate, respectful, inclusive, and everlasting. For, ultimately, God "is the poet of the world, with tender patience leading it by his vision of truth, beauty, and goodness."[11]

NOTES

1. For a general introduction to Whitehead's thought, see John B. Cobb, Jr., and David Griffin, *Process Theology: An Introductory Exposition* (Philadelphia: Westminster Press, 1976).

2. This is what Whitehead called "the reformed subjectivist principle." See Alfred North Whitehead, *Process and Reality* (New York: Free Press, 1969), pp. 182–195.

3. This process is described in greater detail by Whitehead in *Process and Reality,* pp. 251–329.

4. Whitehead calls this function of God "the principle of concretion." See *Process and Reality,* pp. 285–287.

5. See Alfred North Whitehead, *Adventures of Ideas* (New York: Free Press, 1967), pp. 192–194.

6. It is a point of dispute among process theologians whether Whitehead's views allow for subjective immortality. On the negative side see Schubert Ogden, "The Meaning of Christian Hope," in *Religious Experience and Process Theology,* ed. Harry James Cargas and Bernard Lee (New York: Paulist Press, 1976), pp. 195–215. On the positive side see Robert L. Kinast, *When a Person Dies* (New York: Crossroad Books, 1985), pp. 33–46.

7. See Whitehead, *Process and Reality,* p. 341.

8. For a fuller discussion of judgment and suicide from a process perspective, see Kinast, *When a Person Dies,* pp. 60–77.

9. Whitehead, *Process and Reality,* p. 413.

10. This is also the basis for a process interpretation of Jesus' death. See Kinast, *When a Person Dies,* pp. 94–113.

11. Whitehead, *Process and Reality,* p. 408.

Suggestions
for Further Reading

The works listed here include suggestions from all contributors.

Alcohol, Drug Abuse, and Mental Health Administration. *Report of the Secretary's Task Force on Youth Suicide.* Vol. 1: *Overview and Recommendations.* DHHS Pub. No. (ADM) 89–1621. Vol. 2: *Risk Factors for Youth Suicide.* DHHS Pub. No. (ADM) 89–1622. Vol. 3: *Prevention and Interventions in Youth Suicide.* DHHS Pub. No. (ADM) 89–1623. Vol. 4: *Strategies for the Prevention of Youth Suicide.* DHHS Pub. No. (ADM) 89–1624. Washington, D.C.: Superintendent of Documents, U.S. Government Printing Office, 1989.

Alvarez, Alfred. *The Savage God: A Study of Suicide.* New York: Random House, 1972. This moving personal glimpse into the struggle of one engaged in suicidal ideation and activity provides sensitive understanding of suicide dynamics. Perspectives of the study will both challenge and inform the reader.

Battin, M. Pabst. *Ethical Issues in Suicide.* Englewood Cliffs, N.J.: Prentice-Hall, 1982. A thorough discussion of a wide range of topics and cases, with attention to biblical and theological concerns.

———— and David J. Mayo, eds. *Suicide: The Philosophical Issues.* New York: St. Martin's Press, 1980. This volume contains a variety of viewpoints on the deeper philosophical issues posed by suicide. The collection includes the work of Christian ethicists as well as philosophers.

Beauchamp, Tom L., and James F. Childress. *Principles of Biomedical Ethics,* 2nd ed. New York: Oxford University Press, 1983. Suicide is examined in various case studies along with related ethical questions of right to die, family and institutional responsibility, and legal ramifications for state and attending individuals.

Centers for Disease Control. "CDC Recommendations for a Community Plan for the Prevention and Containment of Suicide Clusters." Washington, D.C.: U.S. Government Printing Office, 1988. CDC's recommendations outline coordinated responses for managing crises precipitated by suicides in the community. Guidelines are given to assist clergy, educators, health professionals, and other community leaders in advance planning to identify community resources and designate areas of responsibility. The CDC recommendations provide a reasoned framework that can be adapted locally.

Clemons, James T. *Sermons on Suicide.* Louisville, Ky.: Westminster/ John Knox Press, 1989. A collection of sermons, most of them preached on occasions other than funeral services. A variety of biblical texts, personal illustrations, statistics, and ethical issues. The introduction argues for the need for preaching to help religious communities confront the many issues raised by suicide.

———. *What Does the Bible Say About Suicide?* Minneapolis: Augsburg Fortress Publishers, 1989. An examination of more than ninety biblical texts, with a history of interpretation and a biblical-theological approach to ethical issues.

Faupel, Paul D., Charles E. Kowalski, and Gregory S. Starr. "Sociology's One Law: Religion and Suicide in the Urban Context." *Journal for the Scientific Study of Religion* 26:523–534 (Dec. 1987).

Fedden, Henry Romilly. *Suicide: A Social and Historical Study.* London: Peter Davies, 1938. A classic work of broad subject matter set in major periods of history from ancient Greece through the nineteenth century.

Gibbs, Jewelle Taylor. "Conceptual, Methodological, and Sociocultural Issues in Black Youth Suicide: Implications for Assessment and Early Intervention." *Journal of Suicide and Life Threatening Behavior* 18 (1): 73–89 (Spring 1988).

Gustafson, James. *Ethics from a Theocentric Perspective,* vol. 2. Chicago: University of Chicago Press, 1984. Gustafson is a distinguished scholar and teacher who has written a major work on theological ethics. The chapter on suicide in this second volume is placed within the framework of his constructive interpretation of Christian ethics. Gustafson explores the ethics of suicide with characteristic depth and insight.

Harran, Marilyn J. "Suicide." *Encyclopedia of Religion,* vol. 14, ed. Mircea Eliade. New York: Macmillan Co., 1987, pp. 125–131. An excellent overview of suicide from a variety of major religious perspectives.

Hauerwas, Stanley. "Rational Suicide and Reasons for Living," in *On Moral Medicine: Theological Perspectives in Medical Ethics,* ed. Stephen E. Lammers and Allen Verhey. Grand Rapids: Wm. B. Eerdmans Publishing Co., 1987, pp. 460–466. While this entire volume is helpful on a variety of moral questions related to life and death, the essay by Hauerwas will be of special interest to readers who want to explore the ethics of suicide. Hauerwas's distinctive perspective is clearly presented in this essay: the implications of an ethic of character shaped by the convictions of Christian community for sustaining life and rejecting suicide.

Jackson, Gordon E. *Pastoral Care and Process Theology.* Washington, D.C.: University Press of America, 1981, pp. xiv and 253. This book offers a description of pastoral care from the perspective of process theology. Both the description and the dynamics of pastoral care are reinterpreted in light of process thought. The categories of process thought are explained in clear but technical language.

Kinast, Robert L. *When a Person Dies: Pastoral Theology in Death Experiences.* New York: Crossroad Books, 1984. Using case studies, the author discusses several different types of death experiences, including suicide. In each case the theological questions are identified, a typical explanation is given, and then a process theology interpretation is offered along with a description of its pastoral implications.

Klerman, Gerald L., ed. *Suicide and Depression Among Adolescents and Young Adults.* Washington, D.C.: American Psychiatric Press, 1986. Psychological, biological, and sociological perspectives on suicide are delineated in this balanced volume. Depression and disruptive life events are linked to suicide in the context of typical developmental sequences for young people. The authors review principles of suicide prevention.

Klinefelter, Donald S. "The Morality of Suicide," *Soundings* 57(3): 336–354 (Fall 1984). This essay describes historical and contemporary perspectives on the morality of suicide. The author explores the implications of an ethics of virtue for suicide insightfully; he believes suicide may on occasions be morally appropriate.

Parker, A. Morgan, Jr. *Suicide Among Young Adults.* New York: Exposition Press, 1974. While focusing on young adults, this examination based on clinical research relates dynamics, occurrence, and helpful responses for people of all ages and backgrounds.

Shannon, Thomas A. *An Introduction to Bioethics,* 2nd ed. rev. and

updated. Mahwah, N.J.: Paulist Press, 1987. One of the best collec-
tions of basic writings on ethical questions related to biological possibilities and problems. The section on "Death and Dying"
presents contrasting viewpoints on issues relevant to suicide.

Shneidman, Edwin. *Definition of Suicide.* New York: John Wiley &
Sons, 1985. Demonstrates the importance of clarity in defining the
issues, for rational discussion and even for prevention of suicide.

Sontag, Susan. *Illness as Metaphor.* New York: Farrar, Straus & Gi-
roux, 1978. Perceptions of ourselves and our physical conditions
are discussed so as to remove harmful bias and open channels for
positive, accurate, healing possibilities.

Wogaman, J. Philip. *Christian Moral Judgment.* Louisville, Ky.:
Westminster/John Knox Press, 1989. Explores the problem of
Christian decision-making, with illustrative use of suicide and
euthanasia. Of particular relevance is the analysis of initial presumptions in Christian moral judgment.